October 24–28, 2010
Fairfax, Virginia, USA

**Association for
Computing Machinery**

Advancing Computing as a Science & Profession

SIGAda 2010

Proceedings of the 2010 ACM International Conference on
Ada and Related Technologies

Sponsored by:
ACM SIGAda

In cooperation with:
ACM SIGCSE, ACM SIGAPP, ACM SIGBED, ACM SIGPLAN, ACM SIGCAS, & Ada-Europe

Industrial Supporters:
AdaCore, Ellidiss Software, LDRA, & MathWorks

**Association for
Computing Machinery**

Advancing Computing as a Science & Profession

The Association for Computing Machinery
2 Penn Plaza, Suite 701
New York, New York 10121-0701

ISBN: 978-1-4503-0027-8

Additional copies may be ordered prepaid from:

ACM Order Department
PO Box 11405
New York, NY 10286-1405

Phone: 1-800-342-6626 (USA and Canada)
        +1-212-626-0500 (all other countries)
Fax: +1-212-944-1318
E-mail: acmhelp@acm.org

ACM Order Number 825100

Printed in the USA

Welcome to SIGAda 2010 from the SIGAda, Conference and Program Committee Chairs

Welcome to the 2010 Annual International Conference of ACM's Special Interest Group on Ada (SIGAda), being held in the suburb of Washington, D.C. area, USA at the Hyatt Fair Lakes Hotel. This is a beautiful spot located in Fairfax, Virginia.

This year's conference concentrates on software reliability, safety, and security as among the most critical requirements of contemporary software. The conference starts with two days of multi track tutorials to educate attendees on a variety of technologies to address these same software development topics. This is followed by three days of technical papers, keynotes, and invited presentations. The keynote speakers all have extensive experience in these areas and have been selected to provide attendees with a variety of perspectives on developing high reliability systems. We have a speaker on system software integrity assurance gained from his experience with aviation systems. A second speaker will present his thoughts on the use of Ada in security systems with a specific focus on Tokeneer. We have invited speakers to pass along their experience in developing large scale, high reliability systems. We have introduced three panel discussions as a new edition to this year's conference. Representatives from the US National Institute of Standards and Technology will discuss the potential benefits of software labels. Our second panel will address software security in depth and will be followed by a workshop that should challenge the audience. The final panel will address mitigating risks to the enterprise by software assurance and is moderated by a software leader at the Department of Homeland Security.

During the three days of the main conference schedule you will hear from a variety of presenters that have both project experience and research results in developing highly reliable and secure software. The selected papers were all double blind reviewed to provide you with the very best in presentations for the time you spend at this year's conference. We think many papers will provide information you can directly apply as lessons learned to your own software development projects. Others may be of interest as technologies that have been tested and worth following in the future.

There will be a reception on Tuesday evening to both relax and meet with other attendees to have informal discussions on like minded topics. The reception will be further complemented by the Asian Indian Dance and Music performances. Wednesday evening will have various Birds of a Feather (BOF) sessions arranged around topics of specific interest. Attendees can make the most of their stay and have discussions on topics that directly interest them and are helpful for the work they are performing for their companies today.

Finally, we hope SIGAda 2010 provides you an outstanding opportunity for rewarding affiliation with colleagues in industry, academia, and government — discussions in the hall, informal meal-time meetings, and even during the more relaxed moments we make for socializing in this historic capital city. If you don't realize it already, you will learn that these associations can be as valuable as the technical program at professional conferences, and often extend the experience after you return home.

We take this opportunity to thank our Corporate Supporters as they participate in this year's SIGAda Conference. Our Platinum level supporter is AdaCore. Our Silver level supporters are Ellidiss and LDRA. And thanks to MathWorks for exhibiting.

Table of Contents

SIGAda 2010 Conference Organization vii

SIGAda 2010 Sponsors & Supporters viii

Pre-Conference Tutorials

- **Effective Requirements Engineering** 1
  William Bail *(The MITRE Corporation)*

- **Use of Object Oriented Technologies in High Reliability System** 3
  Jean-Pierre Rosen *(Adalog)*

- **Ada for Parallel, Embedded, and Real-Time Applications** 5
  John W. McCormick *(University of Northern Iowa)*

- **Designing Real-Time, Concurrent, and Embedded
  Software Systems Using UML and Ada** 7
  Robert G. Pettit IV *(The Aerospace Corporation)*

- **Unmanned Systems with Ada and RTEMS** 9
  Cindy Cicalese *(The MITRE Corporation)*, Joel Sherill *(OAR Corporation)*,
  Ricky Sward, Richard Weatherly *(The MITRE Corporation)*

Technical Program

- **Systems Software Integrity Assurance** 11
  Chris Lane *(Lockheed Martin IS&GS)*

- **A Deterministic Run-Time Environment for Ada-05 on the ATmega 16 Microcontroller** 13
  Jim Ras, Albert M. K. Cheng *(University of Houston)*

- **A Methodology for Avoiding Known Compiler Problems Using Static Analysis** 23
  Mamdouh Jemli *(Ansaldo-STS France)*, Jean-Pierre Rosen *(Adalog)*

- **Wouldn't It be Nice to Have Software Labels?** 31
  Elizabeth Fong, Paul E. Black *(National Institute of Standards and Technology)*, Richard F. Leslie *(SCORE)*,
  Simson Garfinkel *(Naval Postgraduate School)*, Larry Wagoner *(Department of Defense)*,
  Gary McGraw *(Cigital)*, Jeff Williams *(Aspect Security)*

- **Experience Report: Ada & Java Integration in the FAA's ERAM SWIM Program** 33
  Richard B. Schmidt *(Lockheed Martin)*

- **"Unmanned Systems and Ada"** 35
  Richard Weatherly *(The MITRE Corporation)*

- **Real-Time System Development in Ada Using Lego® Mindstorms® NXT** 37
  Peter J. Bradley, Juan A. de la Puente, Juan Zamorano *(Universidad Politécnica de Madrid)*

- **Parallelism Generics for Ada 2005 and Beyond** 41
  Brad J. Moore *(General Dynamics Canada)*

- **Extending Ada to Support Multi-core Based Monitoring and Fault Tolerance** 53
  You Li *(Nanjing University)*, Lu Yang *(Soochow University & Nanjing University)*,
  Lei Bu, Linzhang Wang, Jianhua Zhao, Xuandong Li *(Nanjing University)*

- **Towards Ada 2012: An Interim Report** 63
  Edmond Schonberg *(AdaCore, Inc.)*

- **The Rise, Fall and Persistence of Ada** 71
  Ricky E. Sward *(The MITRE Corporation)*

Author Index 75

SIGAda 2010 Exhibitors Guide 77

SIGAda 2010 Conference Organization

Conference Chair:	Alok Srivastava *(TASC, Inc.)*
Program Chair:	Jeff Boleng *(US Air Force Academy)*
Exhibits and Sponsorships Co-Chairs:	Greg Gicca *(AdaCore)* Kristen Ferretti *(OC Systems, Inc.)*
Proceedings Chair:	Clyde Roby *(Institute for Defense Analyses)*
Local Arrangements Co-Chairs:	Avtar Dhaliwal *(Genco Systems)* Florence Gubanc *(OC Systems)*
Workshops Chair:	Bill Thomas *(The MITRE Corporation)*
Publicity Chair:	Michael Feldman *(George Washington Univ., retired)*
Treasurer:	Geoff Smith *(Lightfleet Corporation)*
Registration Chair:	Michael Feldman *(George Washington Univ., retired)*
Tutorials Chair:	Robert Pettit *(The Aerospace Corporation)*
Academic Community Liaison:	Michael Feldman *(George Washington Univ., retired)*
Webmaster:	Clyde Roby *(Institute for Defense Analyses)*
SIGAda Chair:	Ricky E. Sward *(The MITRE Corporation)*
SIGAda Vice Chair for Meetings and Conferences:	Alok Srivastava *(TASC, Inc.)*
SIGAda International Representative:	Dirk Craeynest *(K. U. Leuven, Belgium)*
Program Committee:	Jeff Boleng *(US Air Force Academy)* Julien Delange *(European Space Agency)* Dan Eilers *(Irvine Compiler Corporation)* Mark Gardinier *(Advanced Technologies, Inc.)* John Kassie *(Rockwell Collins)* Gertrude Levine *(Fairleigh Dickinson University)* Sheldon Liang *(Azusa Pacific University)* Stephen Michell *(Maurya Software Inc.)* Karl Nyberg *(Grebyn Corporation)* Jean-Pierre Rosen *(Adalog)* Stephen Schwarm *(S2 Security Corporation)* Dino Schweitzer *(US Air Force Academy)* Frank Singhoff *(European University of Brittany)* Samuel Tardieu *(Telecom ParisTech)*

SIGAda 2010 Sponsors & Supporters

Sponsor:

In cooperation with:

Industrial Supporters & Exhibitors:

Effective Requirements Engineering

William Bail
The MITRE Corporation
McLean, Virginia, USA
wbail@mitre.org

Abstract

Failures in systems closely correlate to shortcomings in the system's requirements. Some historic data suggests that requirements are responsible for nearly half of all system development failures. This is especially true for critical systems that are real-time and embedded. Expectations for fault tolerance, graceful degradation, degraded performance modes, and temporal challenges (latency and synchronization) fail to be fully satisfied by common practice.

This tutorial discusses shortcomings in current practices, and provides guidance for enhanced practices that address historic shortcomings, and provide an approach to weighing tradeoffs associated with ambitious goals and realistic limits. It clarifies terminology to facilitate a clearer focus on underlying concepts. In addition, it specifically addresses the issue of stakeholder acceptability, allowing trade-offs of various system qualities to determine overall system acceptance. The tutorial does not describe in detail any specific techniques. Rather, it describes the ways that requirements need to be handled to maximize the likelihood of success.

The topics covered include:

- An overview of the motivation for why a focus on requirements engineering is important
- A discussion of the fundamental nature of requirements, and an analysis of the different types of requirements.
- A summary of the desired quality attributes of requirements specifications
- An overview of the ways that requirements are defined
- A discussion of the various approaches used for verifying requirements
- A brief analysis of the challenges that present themselves when developing requirements

Categories & Subject Descriptors: D.2.1 Software [SOFTWARE ENGINEERING] Requirements/Specifications: Methodologies (e.g., object-oriented, structured).

General Terms: Documentation, Management.

Use of Object Oriented Technologies in High Reliability Systems

Jean-Pierre Rosen
Adalog
Arcueil, France
rosen@adalog.fr

Abstract

This tutorial presents the new challenges brought by the advent of object oriented technologies (OOT) into the realm of high reliability systems.

For a long time, OOP was deemed too dynamic a model for highly reliable systems, especially levels A/B of the DO178B, although the standard in itself does not preclude the use of any technology. However, interest for introducing OO techniques is growing in the community; the FAA sponsored OOTiA (Object-Oriented Technology in Aviation), a handbook intended to identify and address these issues. Although not an official policy of the FAA, this handbook is a major input for the upcoming revision of DO178B (DO178C).

The tutorial provides an overview of software safety related standards (DO178B in airborne systems, EN5018 for railway systems). Based on the extensive work of the OOTiA, it explains the issues of object oriented technologies in high reliability systems, and how such technologies can be used while ensuring the high degree of control, review, and testing mandated by these systems. Finally, it shows how Ada's object oriented model differs from the traditional model, and brings better solutions for introducing OOP to high reliability systems.

The tutorial will help participants to understand what software safety standards are about, discover the issues of object oriented technologies in high reliability systems, get an up to date view of current trends with regard to OOT and the DO178B, and learn how Ada's model of object oriented programming is especially appropriate for secure systems.

Categories & Subject Descriptors: D.2.4 [SOFTWARE ENGINEERING]: Software/Program Verification – *Reliability*.

General Terms: Design, Reliability, Verification.

Bio

JP Rosen is a professional teacher, teaching Ada (since 1979, it was preliminary Ada!), methods, and software engineering. He runs Adalog, a company specialized in providing training, consultancy, and services in all areas connected to the Ada language and software engineering. He is chairman of AFNOR's (French standardization body) Ada group, AFNOR's spokeperson at WG9, member of the Vulnerabilities group of WG9, and chairman of Ada-France.

Adalog offers regularly on-site and off-site training sessions in Ada. J-P Rosen is a consultant for companies involved in high reliability systems, such as Ansaldo for Railway systems and Thales Avionics for Airborne/OO systems.

Ada for Parallel, Embedded, and Real-Time Applications

John W. McCormick
Computer Science Department
University of Northern Iowa
Cedar Falls, IA, USA
mccormick@cs.uni.edu

Abstract

The arrival and popularity of multi-core processors has sparked a renewed interest in the development of parallel programs. Similarly, the availability of low cost microprocessors and sensors has generated a great interest in embedded real-time programs. Ada is arguably the most appropriate language for development of parallel and real-time applications. This tutorial provides an introduction to the features of Ada that make it appropriate in these domains including:

- High level support for low level programming.
- The task.
- Communication and synchronization based on shared objects.
- Communication and synchronization based on direct interaction.
- Support for compliance with real-time scheduling theory.

Categories & Subject Descriptors: C.3 [Special-Purpose And Application-Based Systems]: Real-time and embedded systems, D.1.3 [Programming Techniques]: Concurrent Programming – *parallel programming*, D.3.3 [Programming Languages]: Language Constructs and Features – *concurrent programming ,structures*, J.7 [Computers in other Systems]: Real time.

General Terms: Performance, Design, Languages.

Bio

John McCormick is Professor of Computer Science at the University of Northern Iowa. He began his career in computer science at the State University of New York in 1979. In 1993 John was awarded the *Chancellor's Award for Excellence in Teaching*. He has served as Secretary, Treasurer, and Chair of ACM SIGAda. He received the *SIGAda Distinguished Service Award* in 2002 and the *SIGAda Outstanding Ada Community Contributions Award* in 2008. He was awarded the *SIGAda Best Paper and Presentation Award* in 1991 and the *Ada Europe Best Presentation Award* in 2008.

John's interests include software quality, the specification, design, and implementation of real-time systems, and the design of courses and laboratories to support teaching of these topics. His real-time model railroad based embedded systems laboratory has been duplicated at schools in North America, South America, Europe, and Australia. He is the major author of *Programming and Problem Solving with Ada* and *Ada Plus Data Structures: an Object-Oriented Approach*. These introductory computer science textbooks are known for their early introduction of software engineering principles. His latest book, *Building Parallel, Embedded, and Real-Time Applications with Ada*, with coauthors Frank Singhoff and Jérôme Hugues is due out this year.

John is a senior member of ACM, a member of SIGAda and SIGCSE, and an affiliate of the IEEE Computer Society.

Designing Real-Time, Concurrent, and Embedded Software Systems Using UML and Ada

Robert G. Pettit IV
The Aerospace Corporation
Chantilly, VA, USA
rob.pettit@aero.org

Abstract

The domain of real-time, concurrent, and embedded software is becoming increasing complex. To effectively develop these systems, greater care must be taken to construct adequate models of the software and to effectively analyze these designs prior to code development. In this tutorial, we will discuss modeling and analysis issues specific to real-time, concurrent, and embedded software systems. Specifically, this tutorial will present guidelines for modeling these systems using the Unified Modeling Language (UML) version 2. A case study will be introduced to solidify the concepts and participant interaction will be encouraged in the construction of the models. Analytical methods will also be discussed to verify that the UML-based designs will produce the desired behavior. Finally, we will discuss how to proceed from the UML models into an Ada (2005) implementation.

Categories & Subject Descriptors: D.2 Software Engineering, D2.2. Design Tools and Techniques (Object-oriented design methods), C.3 Special-Purpose and Application-Based Systems (Real-time and embedded systems)

General Terms: Design, Languages.

Bio

Rob Pettit has over 20 years of experience in the software development industry and is an internationally recognized expert in the field of software design for object-oriented real-time and concurrent systems. Dr. Pettit is currently the co-lead (East) for The Aerospace Corporation's Flight Software and Embedded Systems Office. Additionally, Dr. Pettit serves as an adjunct professor for both George Mason University and Virginia Tech, where he teaches graduate courses in software design and development for real-time, embedded, and concurrent systems.

Dr. Pettit received his B.S., Computer Science degree in 1991 from the University of Evansville, his M.S., Software Systems Engineering degree in 1995 from the George Mason University, and his Ph.D. in Information Technology / Software Engineering from George Mason University in 2003. Dr. Pettit was the General Co-Chair for the Americas of IEEE's 2007 and 2008 International Symposium on Object-oriented Real-time Computing (ISORC 2007 and ISORC 2008) and was General Co-Chair for the 2009 ACM/IEEE International Conference on Model Driven Engineering Languages and Systems (MODELS 2009). Dr. Pettit is a Senior Member of the IEEE; a member of ACM's SIGAda; and a co-author of Ada 95 Quality and Style.

Tutorial

Unmanned Systems with Ada and RTEMS

Cindy Cicalese, Ricky Sward,
Richard Weatherly
The MITRE Corporation
McLean, VA, USA
cicalese@mitre.org, rsward@mitre.org,
weather@mitre.org

Joel Sherrill
The OAR Corporation
joel.sherrill@OARcorp.com

Abstract

This tutorial provides an introduction to the development of software in Ada for unmanned systems. The authors will demonstrate how they are using Ada over RTEMS in developing the real time control software for a large unmanned ground vehicle. RTEMS is an open source, real-time operating system that provides a high performance environment for embedded applications on a range of processors and embedded hardware.

The format of the tutorial will be hands-on, focusing on developing applications in Ada over RTEMS using a live Fedora GNU Linux DVD. The DVD provides a complete GNAT Ada installation with all sources and scripts as well as the prebuilt toolset and simulators. The instructors will demonstrate some of the hardware components of the large unmanned ground vehicle controlled by software developed in Ada over RTEMS. The attendee will gain from this tutorial a practical application of how Ada can be used in the development of unmanned systems. The attendee should bring a x86 compatible laptop with DVD reader, if possible.

Categories & Subject Descriptors: D.2.0 [**Software**]: Software Engineering – *General*

General Terms: Design, Languages.

Systems Software Integrity Assurance

Chris Lane
Lockheed Martin IS&GS
9211 Corporate Blvd., Rockville, MD 20850
001-1-301-640-3547

chris.lane@lmco.com

ABSTRACT

DataComm is a program that will enhance existing communications between the air traffic controller and the pilot by sending digital messages to supplement the existing voice communications. With more reliance on DataComm as the FAA's Next Generation systems become fielded, ensuring the communications is reliable, accurate, and most importantly safe becomes increasingly critical. RTCA DO-278 provides the guidelines for communications, navigation, surveillance, and air traffic management systems software integrity assurance. It doesn't guarantee that the software developed in accordance with these guidelines is safe but if followed it ensures that the processes are in place to properly plan, develop and verify the software. Lockheed Martin is in the process of integrating DataComm with the En Route Automation and Modernization (ERAM) program and is developing the program in compliance with DO-278. This brings challenges as well as opportunities with the increasing reliance on commercial off the shelf (COTS) software. These challenges and some insight into developing systems to the standards of DO-278 will be discussed.

Categories and Subject Descriptors

D.2.0 [**SOFTWARE ENGINEERING**]: General – *protection mechanisms, standards*

General Terms

Design, Documentation, Human Factors, Management, Measurement, Reliability, Security, Standardization, Verification.

Keywords

Software Assurance, Software Integrity, Air Traffic Management, FAA, System Safety, Process

1. INTRODUCTION

This year's conference theme is engineering safe, secure, and reliable systems. Depending on the software application, not achieving these attributes can have impacts ranging from minor inconvenience to world-wide catastrophe. This paper discusses a method of achieving safe and reliable systems being implemented on a Federal Aviation Administration (FAA) program called Data Communications or DataComm which is a ground-based Communications, Navigation, and Surveillance (CNS) Air Traffic Management (ATM) system used for controller – pilot communications.

2. SAFETY AND SOFTWARE PROCESSES

The Radio Technical Commission for Aeronautics (RTCA) working with the aerospace and CNS/ATM industries created safety guidelines for developing software for airborne [1] and CNS/ATM ground systems [2]. These guidelines cover all phases of the software life cycle including the planning, developing, and verifying phases of the process. Through their research, the RTCA identified a strong correlation between the integrity of the systems developed and the thoroughness of the software development process. While it is recognized that following good processes does not guarantee a safe, reliable system, it does provide greater confidence that the software will perform its intended function. These guidelines identify 66 objectives for avionics systems and 78 for CNS/ATM systems which, if satisfied, provide assurance that the software was planned, developed, and verified with the rigor necessary to be used in safety critical operations. The RTCA documents identify which objectives need to be satisfied depending on the needed assurance level. Criticality plays an important part in determining the required assurance level for software. Software criticality is determined by evaluating the impact to the safe provision of service if that service were to fail. One important way to determine this is by performing a hazard analysis on the system in question. Software assurance levels are determined through a safety assessment of the impact of anomalous software behavior which ranges from catastrophic (multiple fatalities) to no safety effect. Since the focus of this paper is on DataComm, a CNS/ATM ground system, the objectives mentioned herein are limited to the CNS/ATM software integrity assurance objectives (DO-278).

2.1 Software Planning Process

The software planning process defines the means of producing software that will satisfy the system requirements. There are 7 objectives to be evaluated including having and following software development plans and software development standards.

2.2 Software Development Process

The software development process, as defined by the software planning process, defines the means for producing code from a set of requirements. The 8 objectives include defining high-level (system), low-level (software), and derived requirements; developing the software architecture; and developing the source and executable code.

2.3 Software Verification Process

The software verification process defines the means for verifying that the software architecture, source code, and executable code meet the specified system, software and derived requirements and that the requirements are accurate and consistent. It includes verifying that the code was developed to the required standards, managing software configuration including problem management, and ensuring software quality assurance processes are in place. There are 45 objectives to be evaluated for the software verification process.

3. ALTERNATIVE METHODS

The software process objectives summarized in the previous section are geared towards software developed to meet specific requirements of a program. In nearly all of these systems, there is a reliance on COTS software to provide some of the processing needs of a program. Whether it's the operating system for the processors or a specific COTS product used in lieu of developed software, COTS software is prevalent and the fact that the development processes used by COTS suppliers are not necessarily consistent with the objectives for software assurance raises the risk of using COTS especially in critical systems. In addition to the software processes above, RTCA has added 11 specific COTS objectives addressing COTS acquisition, requirements, and configuration management. It is often not viable to obtain the necessary objective evidence discussed above from a COTS supplier. It is not likely that the Microsofts, Suns, Googles, and IBMs of the world are going to provide their software development plans and test results in support of a program. The RTCA software assurance documents address the limitations in process assurance when COTS software is used. These include:

- Formal methods – mathematically-based techniques for the specification, development, and verification of software and hardware systems

- Exhaustive input testing – executing a program with all possible combinations of inputs

- N-version programming – multiple, functionally equivalent programs independently generated from the same initial specifications

- Product service history – safety experience with the product including problem resolution and configuration management history

- Architectural protection – reducing the impact COTS failures have on the safe provision of service.

Many of these alternative methods can be cost prohibitive. The next section discusses how COTS assurance is handled on the ERAM program incorporating DataComm functionality.

4. DATACOMM

Lockheed Martin has developed the ERAM system, an air traffic control system used for controlling high altitude flights. ERAM was not developed using the software assurance guidance put forth by RTCA. Nevertheless, subsequent gap analyses show that the ERAM developed software meets the criteria for high assurance levels. However, ERAM uses several COTS products most notably the operating system for the COTS servers. The ERAM COTS suppliers have provided much of the data needed to show their processes meet the objectives for the required assurance level which effectively fills the gaps identified in the gap analyses. Also, extensive service history is available on these products and Lockheed Martin has a battery of tests performed on these products to ensure they meet requirements.

One of the planned enhancements to ERAM is to incorporate DataComm functionality allowing text message communications between air traffic controllers and pilots. Currently, this is done using voice communications. To facilitate DataComm, enhancements are being made to the System Wide Information Management (SWIM) portions of ERAM. The FAA has identified a COTS product to be used for SWIM for message brokering, providing a framework for web services, and performing mediation router functions. We have no service history with the product so are relying on architectural protection schema to address the risk of using this particular COTS product in an environment that requires relatively high levels of software assurance. Fortunately, the COTS product in question primarily performs data routing. To ensure that the COTS product does not modify the content of the data "payload", Lockheed Martin is bracketing the COTS product with a 32-bit checksum. In fact, the 32-bit checksum is to be applied to all communications between Computer Software Configuration Items (CSCIs) to ensure the payload is not modified inappropriately when traversing through the system. While on the subject of adding data to protect data, DataComm uses the FAA Telecommunications Infrastructure (FTI) provided encryption for data traffic entering and exiting the En Route Center. This is added to the many layers of security including firewalls creating "demilitarized zones" or DMZs to isolate the internet traffic from the system providing the service.

5. SPECIALTY ENGINEERING

Reliability, safety, security, human factors, and performance engineering are sometimes collectively known as specialty engineering. There are obvious interdependencies among these disciplines. The software assurance objectives mentioned in this paper to promote safety are intended to improve software reliability as well. A properly designed computer-human interface can increase the likelihood that a user performs the intended task which improves system safety. Security holes in a system can lead to safety issues as hackers can cause denial of service or even take over the systems. As more and more of our systems connect to the internet, the security risk exposure expands to nearly every aspect of our day-to-day lives. Thus, it is extremely important to consider reliability, safety, and security when developing software.

6. REFERENCES

[1] RTCA SC-167. 1992. *Software Considerations in Airborne Systems and Equipment Certification*, December 1, 1992.

[2] RTCA SC-190. 2002. *Guidelines for Communication, Navigation, Surveillance, and Air Traffic Management (CNS/ATM) Systems Software Integrity Assurance*, March 5, 2002.

A Deterministic Run-Time Environment for Ada-05 on the ATmega16 Microcontroller

Jim Ras and Albert M. K. Cheng
Department of Computer Science
University of Houston
Houston, Texas 77004
U.S.A.
jras@acm.org

ABSTRACT

Microcontrollers account for more than 90% of total microprocessors sold, yet their capabilities are seldom explored in computer science courses. A simple 8-Bit microcontroller can be used in a computer language programming course to facilitate the study of computer architecture and fundamental programming concepts. Through hands-on experience, students can appreciate using a computer language such as Assembly or ADA to develop applications for embedded devices. ADA is not often used in small embedded systems because of ADA's high overhead. We can overcome this problem by using a subset of ADA, such as the Ravenscar Profile. The goal of this paper is to describe how ADA can be used to develop high-integrity real-time systems supporting the Ravenscar tasking model of ADA-05 on the Atmel AVR ATmega16 microcontroller. [1]

Categories and Subject Descriptors

D [**Software**]: Miscellaneous;

General Terms

Programming Languages

Keywords

ATmega16, ADA, RTL

1. INTRODUCTION

Microcontrollers are the beating hearts of most systems. Microcontrollers are simple to program, but students most often learn programming in a virtual environment. Moreover, as programming languages become more dynamic and implementations become more complex, students are further removed from the hardware level of the actual machine. This trend will grow dramatically in the coming decade as systems that hide their implementations inside a black box become more complex. This action isolates the underlying hardware from the user. With little or no experience programming at the hardware level, most engineering students graduate with only a sketchy knowledge of the underlying systems.

Many proofs in response time analysis are problematic due to the assumptions on which they are constructed. One such theoretical assumption is that in most cases there are no operating overheads. To ensure that tasks can be scheduled, overheads are often embedded in the worst-case execution time (WCET) of tasks. Most often, performance degradation is the result of the programming language used. For example, while the ADA programming language is often employed in high-integrity systems, the concurrent constructs of the language are often non-deterministic and inefficient. One way to get around this problem is to use different subsets of ADA, such as the Ravenscar Profile [2, 3]. This paper explains, for the first time, how to design an efficient and more deterministic multitasking kernel using the Ravenscar tasking model of ADA-05 on the Atmel ATmega16 [1] microcontroller.

1.1 Organization

Section 2 details the hardware used throughout this study. A comprehensive discussion of the bit manipulation of the I/O ports follows. Section 4 clearly explains the procedure used to programming the ATmega16 microcontroller. Next, we present our method for porting the GNAT compiler. Section 6 introduces a hardware design and implementation project. The final section summarizes this paper's contribution to the advancement of research in this field. It also explores several areas of interest for future research.

2. CHOICE OF HARDWARE

In this paper, we discuss the design and engineering of a custom controller board using the ATmega16 microcontroller. It incorporates the Harvard architecture that physically separates storage and signal pathways for instructions and data. Both the 8-bit and 32-bit AVR processors are based on the Harvard architecture, but are tuned differently for power use and performance. In every Harvard architecture device, the CPU has two busses: one instruction bus where the CPU reads executable instructions and one data bus to read and write the corresponding data. This ensures that a new instruction can be executed in every clock cycle, and eliminates wait states when no instruction is ready to be executed. In all AVR microcontrollers, the busses are wired to give the CPU instruction bus priority access to the on-chip Flash memory, while the CPU data bus has priority access to the SRAM.

The AVR family ranges from 8-pin devices with 1K Flash and 64 bytes of RAM, to 64-pin devices with 128K Flash and 4K of RAM.

---

[1] *Supported in part by the NSF under Award No. 0720856.

The main differences among them are in speed, memory capacity, and I/O capabilities. We selected the ATmega16 for our project because it is a low-power CMOS 8-bit microcontroller. By executing instructions in a single clock cycle, the ATmega16 microcontroller achieves throughputs approaching 1 MIPS per MHz. This allows the student or engineer to optimize power consumption versus processing speed.

The microcontroller is also supported by a full suite of system development tools. Atmel provides a capable assembly language programming environment called AVR Studio that runs under Windows. For this paper, we enhanced the GNAT compiler and used it instead. In vendor-sponsored compiler research projects compilers written by for-profit based organizations perform less efficiently on generic microcontrollers. This is because the compiler can make multiple versions of the code, each optimized for a certain processor and instruction set. In most cases, the system includes a function that detects which type of CPU it is running on, and chooses the optimal code path for that CPU. This is called a CPU dispatcher. CPU dispatchers not only check which instruction set is supported by the CPU, but they also check the vendor ID string. If the vendor string indicates "GenuineX", then the compiler will use the optimal code path. If the CPU is not from the vendor, in most cases, the dispatcher will run the slowest possible version of the code, even if the CPU is fully compatible with a better version.

3. I/O PORTS AND PROGRAMMING

In the ATmega16 microcontroller there are four ports for I/O operations. A port is a group of 8 physical pins on the microcontroller. Note that in Figure 1, of the 40 pins, a total of 32 pins are set aside for the four ports. The four ports are labeled A to D. Each of these pins can be used as Input or Output pins. In order to tell the microcontroller which pin is an input and which is an output, the *DDRx* register must be programmed, where x indicates port A, B, C or D.

```
(XCK/T0) PB0 ⊏ 1      40 ⊐ PA0 (ADC0)
   (T1) PB1 ⊏ 2      39 ⊐ PA1 (ADC1)
(INT2/AIN0) PB2 ⊏ 3      38 ⊐ PA2 (ADC2)
(OC0/AIN1) PB3 ⊏ 4      37 ⊐ PA3 (ADC3)
   (SS) PB4 ⊏ 5      36 ⊐ PA4 (ADC4)
  (MOSI) PB5 ⊏ 6      35 ⊐ PA5 (ADC5)
  (MISO) PB6 ⊏ 7      34 ⊐ PA6 (ADC6)
   (SCK) PB7 ⊏ 8      33 ⊐ PA7 (ADC7)
       RESET ⊏ 9      32 ⊐ AREF
         VCC ⊏ 10     31 ⊐ GND
         GND ⊏ 11     30 ⊐ AVCC
       XTAL2 ⊏ 12     29 ⊐ PC7 (TOSC2)
       XTAL1 ⊏ 13     28 ⊐ PC6 (TOSC1)
   (RXD) PD0 ⊏ 14     27 ⊐ PC5 (TDI)
   (TXD) PD1 ⊏ 15     26 ⊐ PC4 (TDO)
  (INT0) PD2 ⊏ 16     25 ⊐ PC3 (TMS)
  (INT1) PD3 ⊏ 17     24 ⊐ PC2 (TCK)
  (OC1B) PD4 ⊏ 18     23 ⊐ PC1 (SDA)
  (OC1A) PD5 ⊏ 19     22 ⊐ PC0 (SCL)
   (ICP1) PD6 ⊏ 20     21 ⊐ PD7 (OC2)
```

Figure 1. Pin configuration for the ATmega16 microcontroller

The *DDRx* is the Data Direction Register. Writing a "1" to a bit in the *DDRx* makes the corresponding bit an output bit in *port_x*. For example, in ADA we can write:

```
-- alias names for setting the data
-- direction registers
function FF return Boolean renames True;
function Zeros return Boolean renames False;

-- use all pins on PortB for output
```

```
Set (DDRB, (others => FF));

-- use all pins on PortB for input
Set (DDRB, (others => Zeros));
```

To output a "1" on the port bit, the corresponding bit can be set or reset using the *Set_Bit* procedure with the ADA language.

```
-- set a single bit Bit in I/O register Port
procedure Set_Bit (Port:   System.Address;
                    Bit:    Bit_Number;
                    Value:  Boolean);

-- make PORTB bit 1 as "1"
Set_Bit (PORTB, PORTB1_Bit, True);
```

Example. We will briefly examine a case of temporal logic. We will also see that, by using Ada, port addresses can be addressed at the bit level. Let us assume that *PB1* is an input bit and represents the condition of a railroad crossing warning signal. Figure 2 illustrates this example. We begin with a description of the real-time temporal logic of the railroad crossing system.

Specification in English:

Approximately 40 seconds before arriving at the crossing, the train trips a track circuit near the crossing. This triggers the sensor and sends *PB1* high. Whenever *PB1* goes high, a high-to-low pulse is sent to port *C* on the *PC1* bit to turn on the buzzer. The buzzer must sound until the crossing gates are lowered. The crossing gates take 20 seconds to be fully lowered. After the train is detected by the sensor, the train crossing is completed within 90 seconds. The gates rise after the train clears the crossing. [4, 12].

Specification in Ada Real-Time Logic (ARTL):

$\uparrow$ Start of Event, $\downarrow$ End of Event, Time of Event t := @(...);

$\forall i$ @(TrainApproach,i) $\leq$ @($\uparrow$ Buzzer,i) $\leq$ @($\uparrow$ CrossingGate[2],i);

$\forall j$ @($\uparrow$ CrossingGate,j) + 20 s $\leq$ @($\downarrow$ CrossingGate,j);

$\forall k$ @($\downarrow$ CrossingGate,k) $\leq$ @($\downarrow$ Buzzer,k);

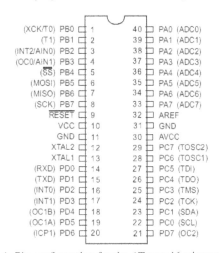

Figure 2. Buzzer Circuit

---

[2]CrossingGate means "the action of lowering the crossing gates."

If the switch is off (open), the input signal is low. The smaller the pull-down resistor, the more voltage goes to ground when the switch is on (closed). Conversely, the larger the pull-down resistor, the less voltage gets 'pulled' to ground and lingers there at the input.

The port addresses are bit-addressable in Ada as follows:

```
-- low level hardware access
with AVR.IO;
use AVR.IO;

-- register descriptions
with AVR.MCU;
use AVR.MCU;

procedure Warn is
begin

  Set (DDRB, (others => DD_Input));
  Set (DDRC, (others => DD_Output));

  -- loop forever
  loop

    -- busy wait until the bit Bit is 1
    Loop_Until_Bit_Is_Set (PORTB, PORTB1_Bit);

    -- make PORTC bit 1 as "1"
    Set_Bit (PORTC, PORTC1_Bit,True);

    -- make PORTC bit 1 as "0"
    Set_Bit (PORTC, PORTC1_Bit,False);

  end loop;

end Warn;
```

4.   PROGRAMMING THE ATMEGA16

The microcontroller can be programmed directly in the target circuit through a JTAG port as shown in Figure 3. JTAG is used for IC debug ports and most modern processors support JTAG when they have enough pins. The great advantage of the JTAG is that it allows for real-time debugging and programming of the microcontroller. Code can be written without mistakes.

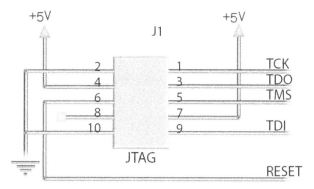

Figure 3. JTAG Port

The JTAG is designed so that multiple chips on a board can have their JTAG lines daisy-chained (Figure 4).

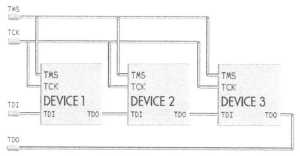

Figure 4. JTAG lines daisy-chained

A test probe need only connect to a single JTAG port to access all the chips on a circuit board. The connector pins are:

1. TCK (Test Clock)

2. TDO (Test Data Out)

3. TMS (Test Mode Select)

4. TDI (Test Data In)

5. RESET

The protocol is serial, so only one data line is available. The clock input is at the TCK pin. It is configured by manipulating a state machine one bit at a time through the TMS pin. One bit of data is sent in and out per TCK clock pulse at the TDI and TDO pins, respectively. The operating frequency of TCK varies depending on the chips in the chain (the lowest speed must be used), but it is typically 10-100 MHz (100-10 ns per bit).

Our target circuit is based on the ATmega16 microchip, but it can be easily adapted to other AVRs. Since the AVR has built-in 1K Byte internal SRAM, 512 Bytes EEPROM, and 16K Bytes of Flash program memory, the minimum external components needed are a crystal, two capacitors and a reset-circuit. The circuit in Figure 5 illustrates how LED's and switches can be connected to the microcontroller.

The eight active-low LEDs are connected to port B and up to eight active-low input switches can be connected to port D. The reset-button is used to manually reset the microchip. The circuit above illustrates the brown-out detector's circuit design, which we will later explain in detail. The detector resets the microcontroller when the power supply voltage is too low. A voltage regulator is used to generate the 5V supply voltage. It is common to use the 7805 chip that can provide up to 1-A output current and can be fed a DC input voltage between 9 V to 20 V.

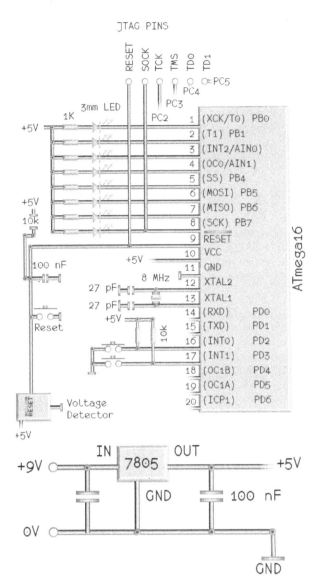

Figure 5. Target Circuit

```
Set (PORTD, FF);

-- use CLK/1024 prescale value
Set (TCCR1B, TMC16_CK1024);
-- reset TCNT1
Set16 (TCNT1, 16#F0BE#);

loop

   -- read input port key that are active-low
   Key := not Get (PIND);
   if (Key and 1) /= 0 then
      LED := 1;
   elsif (Key and 2) /= 0 then
      LED := 2;
   elsif (Key and 4) /= 0 then   -- recognized.
      LED := 4;
   elsif (Key and 8) /= 0 then
      LED := 8;
   end if;
   if Key /= 0 then
      -- Set the correct LED if key pressed
      Set (PORTB, not LED);
   end if;

end loop;

end Main;
```

4.1 Brown-Out Protection

If the power supply voltage is low, the microcontroller may start to execute some instructions incorrectly. To avoid this problem, the CPU must be prevented from executing code during periods of low voltage supply. This is best accomplished by using an external low-voltage detector, also known as a brown-out detector. If the power supply voltage falls below a fixed voltage threshold, the detector forces the RESET pin low (active) and stops the CPU.

Voltage detectors are available as integrated circuits from various semiconductor suppliers. In our circuit we selected a 3-pin fixed voltage detector, the TL7757 from Texas Instruments. The TL7757 is designed for use in microprocessors and monitors the voltage supply for under-voltage conditions. During power-up, when the supply voltage, VCC, attains a value approaching 1V, the RESET output becomes active (low) to prevent an undefined operation. If the voltage supply drops below the threshold voltage level, the RESET output goes to the active (low) level until the supply under-voltage fault condition is eliminated. Any power voltage detector with an active-low open-collector output can be used. The open-collector or open-drain output is required by the ISP-circuit.

5. PORTING THE GNAT COMPILER

In this section, we outline the compiler features that were added to support the Ravenscar tasking model [3] of ADA-05. While ADA is often used for high-integrity systems, the concurrent constructs of ADA have often been defined as being non-deterministic [2]. Advances in scheduling analysis have made it possible to check hard deadlines when using preemptive fixed priority scheduling. This led to the development of the Ravenscar profile, a subset of the ADA tasking model, which was needed to provide the deterministic behavior required to perform scheduling analysis. The following features are supported:

1. Tasks types and objects defined at library level.

To test the circuit in Figure 5, we have created an ADA program that repeatedly turns all the LEDs on and off.

```
with AVR.IO;
use AVR.IO;
with AVR.MCU;
use AVR.MCU;

procedure Main is

   Key : Unsigned_8 := 0;
   LED : Unsigned_8 := 0;

begin

   -- use all pins on PortB for output
   Set (DDRB, (others => FF));
   -- and turn off all LEDs
   Set (PORTB, FF);

   -- set port D for input
   Set (DDRD, Zeros);
   -- setup internal pull-up
```

2. Protected types and objects, defined at library level, limited to one entry having a simple guard and a queue length of one.

3. Ceiling Locking policy with FIFO dispatching policy within priorities.

4. The Ada.Real_Time package for high-precision timing and the *delay until* statement.

5. Synchronous task control, including suspension objects for simple synchronization.

6. Protected procedures as statically bounded interrupt handlers.

Ravenscar defines restrictions to the ADA tasking system and the required dynamic semantics. The restrictions implied by the Ravenscar profile can be designated by the existing definition of pragma Restrictions. The following identifiers apply:

1. No_Task_Hierarchy

2. No_Abort_Statements

3. No_Task_Allocators

4. No_Dynamic_Priorities

5. No_Asynchronous_Control

6. Max_Task_Entries => 0

7. Max_Protected_Entries => 1

8. Max_Asynchronous_Select_Nesting => 0

9. Max_Tasks => N – fixed by the application

The sequential parts of Ada are not affected by Ravenscar. The simplicity of the model allows for the creation of efficient execution-time environments. The Ravenscar version of the ADA Run-Time Library was designed to take advantage of the simplifications allowed by the Ravenscar profile. For example, the GNAT compiler core implements a preemptive fixed priority scheduling with ceiling locking and 256 priorities, including interrupt priorities. In addition, the timing services of the GNAT core provide as high a precision as necessary. This is done by using a 64-bit value for time that is divided into two parts. The less significant part is present in the hardware timer, while the more significant part is stored in memory and is incremented every time the hardware timer overflows.

5.1 Context switching

The GNU ADA compiler (GNAT) is an ADA front-end for the GNU Compiler Collection (GCC). Since both the front-end and back-end are open source components of GCC, porting the GNAT to the ATmega16 architecture was simply a matter of applying some patches. The Ravenscar version of the GNU Ada Run-Time Library (GNARL) is designed to take advantage of the simplifications allowed by the profile. Tasking is simplified since all tasks are at library level, tasks cannot terminate and have fixed priority. Data structures are statically allocated, therefore memory requirements are determined at link time. There were some incompatibilities porting the Ravenscar run-time, but it was easy to fix as we ported the rest of the execution-time environment. Aside from the difficulty in rewriting some of the code, we also had to rewrite how context switching is defined. We wanted to reduce priority inversion, where a higher-priority task must wait for the processing of a lower-priority task.

The process of performing a context switch varies by processor, and some CPUs are set up to handle this rather efficiently. In the typical case, the processor must effectively push the contents of all its registers and flags into RAM, then pop the same type of information for the next task from another RAM storage area. This wastes processor cycles. Our context switch code has less than 40 instructions.

```
.DEF rtptr = R8 ; reg for the running thread adrs
.DEF tstk = Z   ; use Z reg for thread stk ptr
.DEF mpr = R10  ; register for temporary storage
```

The Z register is a particularly convenient register to use for temporary storage. Many instructions make use of the X, Y, and Z registers because they are larger, special purpose registers.

```
/* Get address of running thread */
LDI rtptr, running_thread ; adrs of running thread
LDI tstk, rtptr[0] ; thread code start address
                   ; into the thread stack ptr
```

There are *PUSH* and *POP* commands in the microcontroller instruction set. These make use of the system stack, which behaves exactly like the "thread stack" that we are implementing with the code segment that we have. We could have used the system stack as if it were an interrupt service routine, making the code a bit more straightforward by using *PUSH* and *POP* opcodes. This would, however, have prevented us from using the stack for other purposes that we included in this implementation.

Running_Thread is defined in ADA and is exported to ASM through the *pragma* export feature. The Running _Thread definition is internal to the kernel and is not visible to ADA applications. The address of the running thread is stored in memory instead of being passed as an argument for debugging purposes. The value of the *Running_Thread* is updated each time a new thread gets the processor.

```
/* Save context of running thread */
/* Place thread stack outside prog space */
SUBI tstk, -48
```

This pushes our pointer out and away from the start of the executable code for the thread. We make room by changing the pointer location to 48 memory locations away from the start, thus giving us more than enough room to store all the thread context information.

```
/* Save data registers 0-7 to stack  */
ST -tstk, R0
ST -tstk, R1
```

17

```
ST -tstk, R2
ST -tstk, R3
ST -tstk, R4
ST -tstk, R5
ST -tstk, R6
ST -tstk, R7
```

In these lines, the $R0 - R7$ registers are saved for later with this thread. In this way, the registers can be used again when this thread is loaded. The $-tstk$ simply says decrement the address pointer and load to this memory location. The next load will place register values at the next location and increment again, and so on.

```
IN mpr, SPL   ; read stk ptr (the actual stk ptr)
ST -tstk, mpr ; save on the "thread stack"
```

The opcode *IN* retrieves the value of special registers. In this case, we are reading the value of the Status Register. This command puts it into the designated register. On the next line, we will put this onto our thread stack. When loading, the mirror image of this context is the *OUT* command, which will write information to the special registers, i.e., status register.

We are only using *SPL* (Stack Pointer LOWER) as it is the implementation of the ATmega16 that uses the lower half. Some implementations also use the *SPH* (Stack Pointer UPPER), and, in those cases, they only use the first three bits of this register. If this is the case, we simply add and extra *IN mpr SPH* and *ST −tstk, mpr* to save this information to our stack when we are saving the thread context. We also add the mirror image *LD mpr, tstk* and *OUT SPH, mpr* to retrieve this information from our stack when we are loading the thread context.

```
IN mpr, SREG    ; read status register
ST -tstk, mpr   ; save on the "thread stack"
ST -tstk, R12   ; save R12 to stack

/* Get address of the first thread */
/* Address of first thread code start*/
LDI rtptr, first_thread

/* Put thread executable code start address*/
/* into the thread stack pointer */
LDI tstk, rtptr[0]
```

This is simply a way of loading the running thread address previously stored in $R8$ (we are calling this *rtptr* - or the running thread pointer with the define statement at the top line). The most important thing about the [0] is that it implicitly makes sure that we are getting the address stored in $R8$, and not the value that exists at the address in $R8$.

First_Thread is also defined in Ada and is exported to ASM through the pragma export.

```
/* First thread is now running thread */
ST rtptr[0], tstk ; put address of first thread
                      into running thread pointer

/* Load context of first thread */
LD R12, tstk+ ; load R12 from stack

LD mpr, tstk+ ; load status reg value from stk
OUT SREG, mpr ; replace status reg value
LD mpr, tstk+ ; load stack pointer from stack
```

These commands load the value in *mpr* ($R10$) into the stack (into the address location pointed to by *tstk*). There should also be a sign

at the end of the command to increment the address pointed to after the command completes, ready for the next load at the next location of the stack. Similar to, the description for the above *IN* command, the *OUT* command is used in the load context portion of code to place information into the special registers (i.e., the stack pointer or the status register).

```
/* Replace stack pointer value */
OUT SPL, mpr

/* Load data registers 0-7 from stack */
LD R7, tstk+
LD R6, tstk+
LD R5, tstk+
LD R4, tstk+
LD R3, tstk+
LD R2, tstk+
LD R1, tstk+
LD R0, tstk+
```

The context switch ASM routine is imported to ADA through the pragma Import.

Here is the C language version of the code:

```
/* Get address of running thread */
rtptr = running_thread;
/* Save context of running thread */
//Put thread stack outside program space
tstk = rtptr - 48;

for (i=0; i<8; i++)
{
  // save context (data registers)
  tstk--;
  // save data on the thread stack
  *tstk = data[i];
}
// decrement thread stack address
tstk--;

// save actual stk ptr on thread stack
*tstk = SPL;
tstk--;

// save status register on thread stack
*tstk = SREG;
/* Get address of first thread */
// first_thread is now running
rtptr = first_thread;

/* Load context of first thread */
// load status reg from thread stack
SREG = *tstk;

// increment thread stack address
tstk++;

// load actual stk ptr from thread stack
SPL = *tstk;
tstk++;

for (i=7;i<0;i --)
{
  // load data from thread stk
  data[i] = *tstk;
  // increment thread stack address
  tstk++;
}
```

5.2 Interrupt handling

Interrupt handling is often not predictable. Moreover, the microcontroller has no knowledge of Ada-related priorities. On the ATmega16, all interrupts have a separate interrupt vector in the interrupt vector table. Each interrupt has a priority in accordance with its interrupt vector position. The lower the interrupt vector address, the higher the priority. We modified the compiler to allow different applications to assign different priorities to interrupt groups. Only a simple modification of constants in the specification file and a recompilation is needed to change the priorities.

5.3 Performance

To schedule processes, a scheduler must decide which task is to be scheduled. If the context switch overhead is high, the application performance is degraded. We performed a simple experiment to measure the time needed to switch context. We had one task assert an external pin, unblock a second task and then go to sleep. When the second task started executing, it negated the same pin. The time in which the external pin was asserted was about 25 μs when the system was running at 8 MHz.

6. THE CONTROLLER BOARD

Growing up, most of us were immersed in science fiction. Space travel and laser guns were fascinating, but even more fun were the robots that performed great feats of impossible skill and amazing computations. While this paper will not have you creating anything as complicated as C3PO, or even a R2D2 from Stars Wars, it will show you how to build a controller test board with onboard sensors that could be used to run a Mars Rover, or even a USB missile launcher system.

6.1 Related Work

The controller board that we discuss is similar to a number of controller boards on the market today. They typically include support for a number of analog and digital sensors and interface circuitry for DC motor control. Some examples of these controller boards are the Object-Oriented PIC Board, the Handy Board, and the Parallax Basic Stamp Module. Our controller board combines and enhances many of the ideas presented in the Handy Board [9]. Although the Parallax Basic Stamp [11] module provides excellent software support and a better programming interface, it is not integrated into a controller board which can provide support for direct actuator interfacing, such as for a DC motor. Finally, the Object-Oriented PIC [13] controller board provides a direct interface to the digital I/O pins and provides more servo output ports.

6.2 The electrical design of the system

It is time to apply the knowledge presented here. This section tackles the design of the motherboard for our system. A schematic and lots of hints will turn what could be seen as a difficult process, into something less forbidding. To select a suitable microcontroller, it is important to know the number of I/O ports that are needed. In this controller board there are two outputs per motor (drive and steering), and one to drive an arm. It also needs an input port for an Infrared (IR) sensor to control a wireless robot.

The ATmega16 is an excellent microcontroller for the project. It includes a Master/Slave SPI Serial Interface and a Programmable Serial USART, which is needed to communicate with the sensors.

In Figure 6, of the 40 pins, a total of 32 are set aside for the four ports: *PA*, *PB*, *PC* and *PD*. Each port takes 8 pins. The rest of the pins are used by all series of the Atmel AVR microcontroller. The ATmega16 has an on-chip oscillator but requires an external clock to run it. We used a crystal oscillator and connected it to inputs *XTAL*1 (*pin* 13) and *XTAL*2 (*pin* 12).

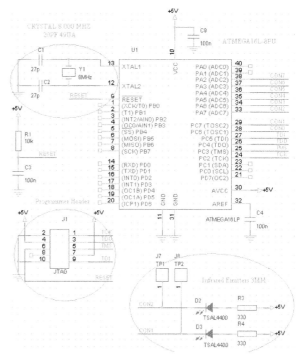

Figure 6. The Microcontroller Board Schematic

CPUs require a reset pulse after the power supply has stabilized. This is to initialize the internal registers and the control circuit. Pin 9 is the RESET pin. The reset sets the program counter (PC) to a predetermined value, for example, PC = 0, causing the microcontroller to start executing our code.

Since the microcontroller has on-board memory that handles the code and data, no external memory chip is required. It is difficult to determine how much program memory will be needed before the code is written. For medium complexity projects, or those with a lot of fixed data (such as text strings or number tables, etc.), 32 to- 40kB is usually enough space. In this project, there is no terminal interface (needing text messages), and there are only a few outputs to control, so we deemed 8kb to be sufficient. The on-chip Flash allows the program memory to be reprogrammed in-system using the JTAG interface. This is done by a conventional non-volatile memory programmer, or by an on-chip Boot program running on the AVR core. The boot program can use any interface to download the application program in the application Flash memory. Software in the Boot Flash section will continue to run while the system Flash section is updated, providing true *Read* − *W hile* − *W rite* operation.

The Infrared (IR) sensor can be done in different ways. To understand this, one needs to know that a typical IR remote produces infrared signals modulated at two frequencies. There is a low frequency data signal (900- 2000Hz) modulated at a fixed high frequency (usually 38 kHz). This is done to prevent false signal triggering from reflection or other devices. To receive the input, a simple two wire phototransistor could be used. This would, however, force the microcontroller to sample the input at a high frequency and do more complicated signal processing, using more program space in the process. A simple 3-wire photo-detector is available that automatically filters out the 38 kHz signal and converts it to a simple low frequency signal. This signal can be fed directly into a UART and read with very little coding.

6.3 Reading the remote control

A used Universal Remote can be purchased at any store. The instruction manual and codes list show how to program the remote. When the IR photo-detector is wired on a breadboard, the output signal can be measured with an oscilloscope. The sensor might not give any readings with the default codes in the remote. This is misleading because it may seem as though the sensor is not working. However, by using an IR phototransistor and watching the high frequency carrier, the frequency can be measured correctly.

The, TSOP34156 IR detector from Vishay is a great general-purpose receiver for IR-based remote-control projects. It is optimized for data rates up to 4000 bits/s and bursts as short as six cycles. The operating voltage range is broad enough for 5 V and 3.3 V logic.

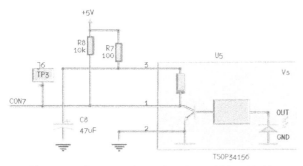

Figure 7. Infrared receiver using the TSOP34156 chip

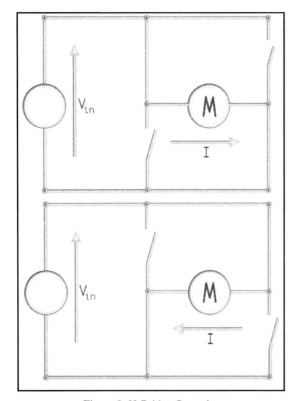

Figure 8. H-Bridge Operation

6.4 Driving the motors

Transistors could be used to drive the motor (as with LEDs), but there are standard chips designed specifically for driving DC motors. The chips used are called H-bridge drivers because they use four drivers with the motor in the middle (looking like an H on a schematic).

Figure 8 illustrates the two basic ways to control the bridge to make the motor go either way. Thus, an H-Bridge is simply a set of four switches with protective flyback diodes.

As illustrated in Figure 9, an L293D control/driver provides a very convenient way to control two motors via a microcontroller chip. Although we did not have many spare parts, we were able to salvage many good pieces from a USB missile launcher which had not worked in many years. Not only did it have two low-voltage DC motors, but there were some useful microswitches that also came in handy. The H-Bridges used (one for each motor) are capable of driving 1A, with 3A peak output.

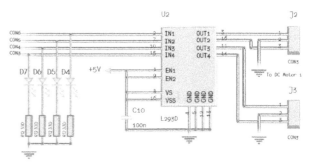

Figure 9. L293D driver for control of DC motors

7. CONCLUSION

In this paper, we described how a deterministic multi-tasking run-time environment supporting the Ravenscar tasking model of ADA-05 is implemented on the Atmel ATmega16 microcontroller. The simplicity of the ATmega16 microcontroller facilitates the design of high-integrity real-time applications. In particular, the context switch and interrupt handling procedures are simplified. The context switch run-time is efficient and constant. It is deterministic easing schedulability analysis. It avoids the problem of having a worst-case execution time that is significantly longer than the average-case. This makes it easier for us to study how real-time applications can be scheduled.

Our future goals include testing our code on other microcontrollers. Additionally, we hope to incorporate real-time temporal logic as an extension of ADA. Success in this venture could broaden ADA's use.

Acknowledgments

The successful completion of the paper would have been impossible without the referees, whose recommendations have greatly enhanced both its clarity and accuracy. Their guidance has been invaluable, and we incorporated their suggestions for improvement each year.

8. REFERENCES

[1] Atmel Corporation. (2008, June 25). AVR 8-bit RISC, [online] at http://www.atmel.com/products/avr/.

[2] Burns A., Dobbing B., and Vardanega T. Guide for the use of the Ada Ravenscar profile in high integrity systems. Ada Letters, vol. XXIV, no. 2, pp. 1-74, 2004.

[3] Burns A. The Ravenscar profile. Ada Letters, vol. XIX, no. 4, pp. 49-52, 1999.

[4] Cheng A. Real-Time Systems: Scheduling, Analysis, and Verification, John Wiley and Sons, 2nd printing with updates, 2005.

[5] The Free Software Foundation (FSF), [online] at http://www.fsf.org/.

[6] Community devoted to the AVR processors, [online] at http://www.avrfreaks.net /.

[7] Gregertsen K. and Skavhaug A. A Real-Time Framework for Ada 2005 and the Ravenscar Profile. 35th Euro. Conference on Software Engineering and Advanced Applications, 2005.

[8] Gregertsen K. and Skavhaug A. An efficient and deterministic multi-tasking run-time environment for Ada and the Ravenscar profile on the Atmel AVR. EDAA, 2009.

[9] Martin F. The Handy Board Technical Reference, [online] at http://www.handyboard.com/.

[10] Mezzetti. E., Panunzio M., and Vardanega T. Preservation of Timing Properties with the Ada Ravenscar Profile. Reliable Software Technologiey - Ada-Europe, pp: 153-166, 2010.

[11] Parallax Inc. BASIC stamp microcontroller, [online] at http://www.parallax.com/.

[12] Ras J. Programming the AVR Microcontroller. USC Technical Report, 1996.

[13] Savage Innovations. The Object-Oriented PIC, [online] at http://www.oopic.com/.

[14] Vardanega B. Automated model-based generation of Ravenscar-compliant source code. Proceedings of the 17th Euromicro Conference, pp: 59-67, 2005.

A Methodology for Avoiding Known Compiler Problems Using Static Analysis

Mamdouh Jemli
Ansaldo-STS France
4, avenue du Canada
91944 LES ULIS CEDEX
FRANCE
+33 (1) 69 29 62 74
Mamdouh.JEMLI@ansaldo-sts.fr

Jean-Pierre Rosen
Adalog
19-21 rue du 8 mai 1945
94110 ARCUEIL
FRANCE
+33 (1) 41 24 31 40
rosen@adalog.fr

ABSTRACT

EN-50128, the European standard for railway software safety, requires that software be demonstrated as free from using language features that would trigger known bugs in the compiler.

Given a list of problem reports provided by the compiler vendor, this paper presents a methodology to achieve this goal by identifying conditions that are *sufficient* to prove that the problem does not happen, and then using a static analysis tool to verify the sufficient conditions.

The methodology has been used and accepted for the certification of SIL4 software, the highest certification level for railway systems.

Categories and Subject Descriptors

D.2.4 [**SOFTWARE ENGINEERING**]: Software/Program Verification – *Reliability.*

General Terms: Measurement, Reliability, Verification.

Keywords: Ada, safety high reliability systems, Ada 2005, Static analysis, AdaControl.

1. INTRODUCTION

Ansaldo-STS is developing complex railway systems used by metros, conventional trains, and TGVs (high speed trains). These include board and ground systems, and many of these systems are written in Ada, and have to be certified at SIL4 level, the highest Safety Integrity Level as defined by the applicable standard for railway systems, EN-50128 [2].

One of the requirements of EN-50128 is that the software shall exhibit deterministic behavior, and thus requires the use of certified compilers and safety analysis of the known problems in the compiler. The certification documents should provide evidence that the software does not exercise any known problem or defect in the compiler, something which, in practice, can be quite difficult to achieve.

Ansaldo-STS awarded a contract to Adalog to define a process to that effect, and analyze several of its programs. This paper presents the methodology that has been designed, using static analysis and Adalog's "AdaControl" tool [3].

2. KNOWN PROBLEMS IN COMPILERS

It is a fact of live that compilers, like any piece of complex software, have remaining defaults and can fail to generate proper code. Certification suites, like the ACATS for Ada, are intended to check the conformity of the compiler to the standard, but not specifically to search for compiler bugs.

For airborne software, according to DO178B, a tool whose usage affects directly the generated code has to be certified to the same level as the code it is used for, or the generated code should be manually verified[1]. For railway systems, EN50128 does not have such a requirement, but requires evidence that the software does not use any language feature which is known to trigger the generation of defective code by the compiler.

However, identifying which language constructs can lead to errors in code generation is far from being simple. Today's compilers are very mature, and the contexts in which problems may happen are generally very complex, implying a combination of features. Simply understanding the issue can require a good expertise in the language, as in the following example:

> *Wrong code may be generated for calls to subprograms when the actual parameter corresponding to a constrained array formal parameter is an aliased array of a constructed subtype whose nominal subtype is unconstrained.*

In general, a problem in a compiler is discovered and identified following a complaint from a customer. An ideal customer provides a well reduced example of how to trigger the bug. This allows the vendor to identify the origin of the problem and provide a fix for the defective code, which will be included in the next release of the compiler (or provided to the customer as a wave-front version if the defect resulted in a blocking problem).

It seems that the best strategy for a customer would be to always use the latest version of the compiler. However, industrial constraints often prevent from switching compiler versions too often: the effort for updating all workstations can be significant, certification of software using the new version must be redone form scratch, etc.

---

[1] Which assumes that manual inspection is more reliable than automated tools – which can be considered a dubious assertion.

Moreover, a new version of the compiler normally includes various improvements, which in turn can introduce new (and unknown) defects. Therefore, most projects use a baseline version of the compiler, and stick to it even in the presence of known problems.

In addition, vendors generally provide work-arounds to avoid the occurrence of identified deficiencies. This makes avoiding the situation quite straightforward once it has been identified.

For these reasons, the most frequent situation is that the client uses a compiler which is not the most current one. This gave time to identify possible defects of the compiler, and it must therefore be demonstrated that the software does not step upon a known defect.

3. A METHODOLOGY FOR AVOIDING KNOWN PROBLEMS

In this part, we are assuming that the compiler vendor provides a list of known problems that accurately describes the circumstances that can lead to the problem; we will discuss in section 6 the extent to which such a list can be trusted in practice. According to the terminology used by the Gnat compiler, each description is called a Known Problem Report, or KPR in short.

The goal of the methodology is to produce a safety analysis report that can be provided to certification authorities to show that each KPR has been addressed, and either is not safety-critical, or has been shown with sufficient evidence as not happening in the code under inspection. The report is then included as part of the certification package for the software.

The methodology proceeds in several steps:

1) Determine which KPRs affect safety and need to be checked.

2) Using the notion of *sufficient condition*, define a set of restrictions (i.e. language features that should not be used) to guarantee that no known compiler problem is exercised

3) Use tools or tool-assisted manual inspection to ascertain the absence of use of the restricted features.

3.1 Classification of the safety impact of Known Problem Reports

The first step consists in classifying the KPRs according to their effect regarding safety. The list of KPRs as provided by the vendor is imported into a spreadsheet, and reviewed by an expert to decide which KPR affects safety, and which do not.

A KPR affects safety if it can result in a program that executes, but does not behave as intended from the source code. Typically, KPRs that do *not* affect safety are related to:

o Problems whose effect is to prevent the compiler from terminating normally (compiler "bombs").

o Problems whose effect is to reject a legal program.

o Problems that result in unnecessary recompilations.

o Problems that prevent correct binding or linking of the program.

o Problems that exist only for a specific target computer and/or operating system, and these are not the ones used by the software.

o Problems that result in incorrect warnings from the compiler, while the generated code is correct

o Problems that do not prevent the generation of the executable, but prevent the program from starting.

o Problems that lead to inefficient, but not incorrect code, time-wise or memory-wise (provided the real-time constraints and space requirements of the project are still met).

o Problems that affect only the operation of external tools, like debuggers or ASIS applications.

o For programs that never stop (as is often the case for real-time programs), problems that show up only at termination, or prevent the program from terminating normally.

Any KPR where it is not 100% clear that it cannot affect safety (including the cases where the description is unclear or insufficient) is classified as affecting safety. For example, some KPRs refer to illegal code that is not rejected by the compiler as it should according to the standard, like in the following example:

Compiler fails to reject an extension aggregate for a non-derived type when the ancestor part names the type itself.

Although this is generally due to obscure legality rules, and the generated code is likely to correspond to the programmer's expectations, these *are* considered as affecting the safety, since there is no officially defined behavior for such programs (and of course, no corresponding executable test in the ACATS).

KPRs classified as "not affecting safety" are ignored, in the sense that no further analysis is needed on the client's code; however, the safety analysis report lists all KPRs and, for the non safety-critical ones, justifies why the KPR is being ignored. Note that KPRs that have no effect on safety may still represent a serious nuisance to the user!

3.2 Analysis of remaining KPRs for a sufficient condition

As mentioned above, problems in compilers happen only on very precise (and rare) conditions, involving the conjunctions of several factors. Each of these factors is a *necessary* condition for the KPR to happen. Since the goal of the study is to prove the *absence* of constructs that would trigger the compiler bug, it is sufficient to show that one of the conditions that make up the problem is never used in the code. We call such a condition a *sufficient* condition for the KPR. Of course, there are generally several possible sufficient conditions for any given KPR, but the *absence* of a condition is sufficient to prove that there is no occurrence of the KPR.

The next step of the methodology consists in reviewing all KPRs that may affect safety and determining a sufficient condition for each. A good sufficient condition must meet several requirements:

o It must be strict enough to be effectively discriminatory, i.e. it must correspond to a feature that is effectively not otherwise used in the program. This largely depends on the application, and "strict enough" can be quite large in practice. For example, if a KPR relates to tasking and the application is known to not use tasks, a sufficient condition will be "no declarations of tasks".

o It must be wide enough to cover a maximum of KPRs. If a condition can be found that is sufficient for several KPRs, this will reduce dramatically the number of checks that need to be performed, and hence the validation effort.

o It must be easily checkable by automated tools (more on this later). This depends of course of the tools that are available, but if several sufficient conditions are possible for a given KPR, preference should be given to the one that is more conveniently checked by tools. This reduces the cost and increases the reliability of the checking, as compared to manual inspection.

o   As far as possible, it should involve the checking of a single language feature. While tools can easily detect the use (or absence thereof) of a feature, it is very difficult to check the simultaneous occurrence of two different features related to the same construct.

Note that although most sufficient conditions are the absence of certain language features in the program itself, some of them may be related to external properties, like the build process. For example, some KPRs happen only with certain levels of optimization. If the build process for the project uses a different optimization level, a sufficient condition is simply to not use the failing level for any compilation.

3.3 Verifying the sufficient conditions

Once a list of sufficient conditions has been established, the next step consists in checking the code to verify that all sufficient condition are indeed absent from the code, and therefore that the code is free from any KPR instance. Of course, every condition must be actually checked; for example, simply stating "we are not using tasking in this program" would not convince the safety authorities: a proof that tasking is not used is required.

In practice, such a check would be impossible to perform manually. For other kinds of safety reviews, an inspections often consists in showing that some elements are indeed present in the code; a report can then be issued that refers to those elements, and the report can be checked by the certification authorities. A human omission would result in a false positive – a place which is correct but marked as missing, involving no safety hazard. But in the case of KPRs, we are looking for the *absence* of certain features; an omission would result in a false negative, which is not acceptable in a safety critical context. And how could you convince the certification authorities that every statement has been correctly inspected?

Therefore, the verification step must be automated, and has to rely on tools. There are two important preconditions that are required for the verification to be effective:

o   The program must be compilable.

o   The verification is run on the whole, complete, program.

On the other hand, nothing *more* can be asserted than the fact that the whole program compiles correctly. This rules out all textual search tools, like *grep* and the like, even for simple cases. Consider for example the condition: "the package Ada.Strings.Unbounded is not used". It would be very difficult for textual tools to recognize a **with** clause for that package, if it is written as:

```
with
  Ada   -- A comment
  .

  Strings -- Another comment
  -- and another one with semi-colon;
  .

  Unbounded

  ;
```

Of course, when dealing with safety issues, the argument that "nobody writes code like this" is not acceptable, as soon as the code is legal Ada. And searching for "unbounded" alone is not acceptable

either, since there can be local identifiers by that name, or the name may appear in comments or character strings.

A perfect verification tool would offer a standard check that corresponds exactly to each sufficient condition; the verification would then be completely automated. In practice, it happens quite often that a standard check can be found; since there is a lot of flexibility in the choice of the sufficient condition, it is easy to select a condition that matches the possibilities of the tool.

For example, many KPRs refer to a bug in the implementation of a language-defined package. The sufficient condition in this case will be the absence of a **with** clause for the package, provided the package is not otherwise used. If the package is used, but the KPR involves a single subprogram from the package, the condition can be made stricter by checking only calls to the failing subprogram[2]. In general, any condition that involves the use of a feature which is known to be unused (maybe because it is forbidden by the coding standard), like tasks, protected objects, tagged types, controlled types, etc., can be easily checked.

But sometimes, a KPR happens only for a combination of features, and all of them are used (but not at the same time) in the program. Picking up any of these features as a sufficient condition will trigger *false positives*: cases that are flagged while not meeting all the conditions for the KPR to happen.

What is really needed at that point is the ability to detect the combination of several features; but it is highly unlikely that any standard check provided by a tool can identify a combination of features corresponding exactly to the context of a KPR. In that case, two possibilities remain:

o   if the tool is open source and allows the development of new checks, the detection of the combination of features can sometimes be added to the tool as a new rule. Although this approach may seem extreme (developing a new rule for just one purpose), it can be cost-efficient in some cases, since the development of a rule can cost much less than the manual inspection it replaces.

o   otherwise (if the tool cannot be extended, or if such extension is deemed too costly or impractical), the tool can still be used to provide *manual-assisted* verification. The idea is that an (insufficient) condition is checked by the tool, therefore identifying potential places where the KPR could happen, and then manual inspection is used to rule out the other conditions. Although there is still a manual check, it is much less error-prone than a fully manual check, since it is limited to (hopefully) a small number of potential places. The certification report can then easily show that each of these places has been correctly inspected, therefore making sure that no suspicious place is forgotten.

Note that any place where the tool signals the occurrence of a sufficient condition needs to be manually inspected[3]. There is therefore no need to distinguish between cases that were intended to be "manual-assisted", and cases that were expected to never happen: all of them must be reviewed – and justified.

---

[2] But more difficult to check: the tool must now consider visibility rules, overloading, renamings, derived subprograms…

[3] Remember that it is the *absence* of a sufficient condition that guarantees that the KPR is not present.

Therefore, the process of verifying the conditions will involve a combination of tools and manual inspection. Choosing the right tool(s) is of paramount importance for the ease of verification and the confidence that all cases are effectively correctly diagnosed, and for reducing manual inspection to an acceptable number of cases.

In practice, it must be understood that the set of sufficient conditions identified by the first pass of analysis will generally leave too many cases to manual inspection. Therefore, the selection of sufficient conditions and the checking of the conditions over the code, form an iterative process. For example, a number of KPRs are related to protected types. A first application that we checked did not use any protected type, therefore checking the absence of protected types was a sufficient condition for several KPRs. However, when the methodology was applied to a different piece of software, a protected type was used to handle interrupts; it was therefore necessary to define another (and less easily checkable) sufficient condition. Alternatively, if there are very few protected objects, leaving the check for protected objects and checking manually that the other conditions did not apply (i.e. turning the check to manual-assisted) could have been a practical solution.

4. THE METHODOLOGY IN PRACTICE

4.1 The checking tool: AdaControl

The tool we chose for cheking the conditions was AdaControl[4] [3]. AdaControl is Adalog's Ada source controller program. It is free software, while still being a commercial product of Adalog [4].

AdaControl inspects a set of Ada source files for occurrences of language features, special constructs, or programming patterns, according to a rules file that defines which controls[5] must be performed. At the time of writing, AdaControl offers 388 rules and subrules, most of which can be parameterized.

The main usage of AdaControl is for verifying coding standards, by providing controls that correspond to constructs that are not allowed by the coding rules. But AdaControl is more general than a simple rule checker: it can detect many programming patterns for other purposes, like in the case described in this paper, where it has been used to identify violations of the sufficient conditions.

AdaControl is based on ASIS [1]; this ensures that it handles the program the same way that the compiler does, and especially that it can handle renamings correctly, which are a common pitfall for many checking tools.

An interesting feature of AdaControl is its extendibility; as most free software, it is available as source code, and it has been designed in a way that makes it easy to add new rules for special purposes. Moreover, new controls can be added as regular rules if the check is deemed general enough to be useful for other purposes, or as a specific rule whose only purpose is to check exactly the required condition.

AdaControl has other features that make it especially suitable for safety analysis: it provides a rule that makes sure that the analyzed code is complete (i.e. it signals any unit withed by another unit and not analyzed), and a rule that reports any check that could not be

performed due to the limitations of static analysis (i.e. when the check depends on run-time conditions).

4.2 Automating the verification process

The verification process for any kind of safety assessments should avoid manual steps as much as possible. Everything performed manually is subject to errors, omissions, etc., and it is hard to prove (and convince the certification authorities) that the manual inspection was performed exactly as described in the inspection procedures.

In our case, we developed a single script to run the whole verification. The script takes a single argument: the name of a directory containing all the sources under inspection. The script performs various sanity checks and runs AdaControl with a rules file that produces three result files: one for fully automatic checks, in CSV format, and two for manual-assisted checks, in CSV and Gnat format.

The CSV files can be easily loaded in a spreadsheet that produces statistics about failed checks (if any). For manual-assisted checks, the spreadsheet provides a column to be ticked by the inspector (with proper justification) for each potential problem.

The file in Gnat format can be loaded in a development environment such as AdaCore's GPS in the "locations" window. The inspector can then use the features of the IDE for browsing the places that need manual inspection, just as conveniently as usually done with compilation error messages.

4.3 Validating the verification process

The verification process involves running one, or sometimes several tools. In addition to the tools themselves, the verification process involves various scripts, parameterizations, etc.

In a highly secure system, anything used towards the certification of software must be shown to be reliable. Therefore, a test suite has been designed, with a test program that reproduces the context of every KPR classified as affecting safety. The same scripts used for the verification are run against this test suite, and the same spreadsheet is used. The corresponding results are attached to the report, showing that every KPR is correctly diagnosed and reported by the verification scripts.

In addition, AdaControl is provided with its own full unit-testing suite, and a stress test that consists in running all AdaControl rules against all the executable tests of the ACATS to increase confidence in the realiability of AdaControl itself.

Note that since AdaControl is free software, the certification authorities can review the source code for the tool itself, should they wish to do so[6].

4.4 Documentation

In order to be able to reuse the analysis framework on various projects, we have separated the documentation in two kinds of documents: the analysis guides, and the verification reports.

There is one analysis guide for each version of the compiler (and therefore for each list of KPRs). This guide presents the methodology, summarizes the justifications for the classification of KPRs, and serves as a user's guide for running the verification,

---

[4] To be honest, this was not really a choice – Adalog was awarded this contract thanks to proposing the possibilities of AdaControl.

[5] According to AdaControl's terminology, a *control* is the application of a *rule* with provided parameters.

[6] They usually don't, but knowing that it is possible increases the confidence in the tool.

including the validation of the verification process itself. Directions are detailed for the manual verifications, where manual-assisted checks are necessary.

There is one verification report for each application that has been submitted to verification. It identifies the software, the version of the compiler, provides the result of running the process, and gives the justifications for every manual-assisted checks that was identified by the tool. In the conclusion, it asserts that no known KPR has been found in the software[7].

5. EXEMPLES

Following are examples of KPRs, how the sufficient condition was selected, and how it translated in AdaControl's terms.

First, here are some examples of KPR that were not classified as affecting safety:

An incorrect warning that Current_Task should not be used and that Program_Error will be raised is issued when a call to Current_Task occurs as the default expression of the formal of an entry body.

(no effect on generated code)

Compiler aborts on a formal package when the generic package has a formal that is an abstract subprogram and the formal package has a box initialization for it.

(no code generated)

GDB fails to provide the contents of the variant part of a record whose type is the subject of an Unchecked_Union pragma, and sometimes crashes displaying it.

(affects the debugger only)

Here is an example of an easy KPR:

Incorrect Decimal_IO output with Aft=0, Exp>0

Since the KPR talks about an "incorrect" result, it is classified as affecting safety. However, we knew that Decimal_IO was not used in the project. Therefore, the sufficient condition is simply:

Check that Decimal_IO is not used.

which in turn can be translated into a control for AdaControl (this would report any use of Decimal_IO, even through renamings):

```
check entities (Ada.Text_IO.Decimal_IO);
```

Here is a slightly more sophisticated example:

A procedure of the form "procedure p is begin p; end;" is incorrectly optimized away to be equivalent to a null procedure.

This was considered affecting safety, because such a procedure body could be automatically generated by a development tool or IDE. If the user forgets to implement the body, it would normally result in infinite recursion that should be easily diagnosed during testing. But due to the KPR, the effect of the procedure would be to

silently do nothing, and this could easily go undetected[8]. Therefore, the sufficient condition was:

Check that the statements of a procedure body do not include only a call to itself, and that the statements of a function body do not include only a return statement whose expression is a call to itself.

(Although the KPR mentioned only procedures, we generalized it to functions, since it is the case where the construct is generated automatically by the GnatStub tool). There was initially no rule in AdaControl to recognize this construct; however, we felt that there was value for detecting this, even if not in the context of searching for KPRs, since it is quite common to forget to implement a subprogram. We added therefore the corresponding control to the general rules of AdaControl. The check is simply:

```
check declarations (self_calling_procedure,
                    self_calling_function);
```

Here is one that required additional manual inspection:

Incorrect code may be generated on assigning or comparing a slice of a composite component of a record for which a component clause specifies a non-byte aligned location in the record.

It is a typical case of a combination of features: the problem happens during a slice assignment, but only if the array component is of a record type, and non-aligned. It was not possible to define a simple sufficient condition, and developing a special rule for this case seemed too complicated; since there was already an AdaControl rule checking various conditions on representation clauses, we extended it to check arrays with unaligned components:

```
check representation_clauses
      (array non_aligned_component);
```

If this rule is triggered, manual inspection will check if the component is of a record type. If not, there is no issue. If it is, cross-references will be used to check that no slice of an array variable of this type is taken.

Here is a KPR where the sufficient condition involved the build process:

When -fstack-check is specified, wrong code may be generated or aggregate assignments or declarations of aggregate using an aggregate value if they involve function calls.

The sufficient condition was simply:

Do not to use the –fstack-check option.

(we knew that it was already the case anyway). In practice, since the whole regular build process also used scripts, the check consisted in a manual inspection of the scripts.

Finally, a complicated one. The KPR, as initially stated, said:

---

[7] Of course, if KPRs *are* found, they are fixed, and the process is run again until it passes.

[8] The latest versions of GnatStub insert a "**raise** Program_Error" in automatically generated bodies, making less likely that such omissions get undetected.

An assignment to a 48-bit standalone variable of a record type with size+representation clauses writes 64 bits instead of 48 when the source of the assignment is a component reference nested within an outer record with size+representation clauses as well, nested in turn within a packed array with size clause.

The KPR was clearly affecting safety, since it lead to memory overwrites. Actually, the problem had occurred previously in the application, and found during testing. However, in reviewing the case, it appeared that the variable that was assigned to had a size that was not 48 bits! This was a case where the KPR reported the circumstances where the problem had been identified, but the problem could happen in more general cases. Taking advantage of the maintenance contract, we asked the vendor for more details, and the KPR was further explained as:

- *you must have an assignment of a value of a type T*

- *T'size must be < 64 and different from any of (8, 16, 32, 64)*

- *the lhs (left hand side of the assignment) must be non "packed" (for instance a standalone variable of type T or a field of a non "packed" record)*

- *the rhs must be a record component reference nested in an outer record which itself is "packed" directly or indirectly.*

This was typically a case of interaction of several features. The simplest sufficient condition we could achieve was:

Check that no record of non-standard (8, 16, or 32 bits) size with less than 64 bit, used as component of a packed structure, is assigned to an unpacked variable.

But still, this condition failed the single feature criterion. A single criterion could have been "check assignment to unpacked variables", or "check assignment from packed type", but these would have make too many false positives to be usable.

Therefore, we developed a custom AdaControl rule to check that particular KPR. For every assignment, the rule checks (in order):

o   That the LHS is packed;

o   That the RHS is of a record type;

o   That the RHS is a record component;

o   That the enclosing record of the component is packed;

o   That the size of the type of the component is less than 64 bits, and different from 8, 16, and 32 bits.

Of course, as soon as a condition is false, further analysis can be abandoned. Therefore, the checks are ordered in a way that eliminates most cases very early, and where the costly checks are done last. Although the test looked quite complicated, the rule did not show any significant performance hit during the verification.

Note that occurrences of this KPR would be very hard to find by manual inspection. When the process was initiated, the methodology was expected to provide better confidence in the code, but it was not expected to find any real problem, since the software had already undergone extensive testing and validation. However, the process discovered an instance of this KPR that had survived all run-time tests, showing the value of the methodology.

6. DIFFICULTIES AND LIMITATIONS

The starting point of the methodology is the description of known problems, as reported by the compiler vendor. The accuracy of this description is therefore extremely important: if the description is too vague, imprecise, or overly general, there is little hope of obtaining any sensible sufficient condition.

Some compiler vendors provides a detailed list of known problems for each version of the compiler (and especially AdaCore for the GNAT compiler, following the general openness philosophy of the compiler); this list provides a sound basis for the analysis of KPRs. But some vendors have not (or do not want to make publicly available) such a list. In this case, the problems have to be deduced from the list of "fixed issues" from the next release of the compiler. Such a list is often not detailed enough to determine precisely what the problem was. For example, statements like "fixed a race condition in protected types" is clearly insufficient for any formal verification. Moreover, if several releases have appeared since the one used in the project, it raises the question of problems listed for version N+2: were they already in version N, or did they appear in version N+1?

Even with a precise list of KPRs, it may happen that a problem occurs in such obscure cases that it is not possible to determine precisely the circumstances that could lead to the error, such as in the following KPR:

In very rare cases, the result of dividing one 64-bit fixed-point type by another may be incorrect. We have not been able to demonstrate a specific example, but an obscure error in one of the run-time library support routines used in this case has been found and fixed, so it is likely that there do exist some cases where this bug is triggered

But sometimes, the description is *too* accurate; it describes the precise context in which the problem was discovered, but the bug in the compiler could have caused the problem in some different contexts, that were never discovered before the bug was fixed. In the last example above, a problem was discovered by software testing, and related to a KPR, although it occurred in a context that was slightly different from the provided description; the corresponding sufficient condition was too narrow, and the problem was not identified by the process. This was reported to the vendor, who provided a more accurate description of the issue. Once the issue was better understood, the test was widened, and the failing occurrence correctly flagged.

Even when an appropriate description of the KPRs is provided, the analysis of the compiler problem and the determination of a sufficient condition require the services of an expert in programming languages, compiler technology in general, and the possibilities of the verification tool.

On the other hand, once the scripts for running the verification have been prepared, with correct parameterization of the tool, running the verification process can be done as part of the routine development process. If the static analysis tool is properly integrated in the development environment, it can be run on any new piece of software, before entering the testing phase. This saves a lot of effort, since bugs due to compiler errors are often very difficult to identify.

Compiler vendors are sometimes reluctant to providing an accurate list of KPRs, because they fear the legal liability that could be incurred if an accident was caused by an unreported compiler bug.

However, it is clear that the EN-50128 standard only requires the checking of *known* problems; in a compiler, like in any sophisticated piece of software, there are also *unknown* problems – and nothing can be asserted for them.

It should therefore be understood that the required process, and the methodology we present here, are not claiming to prove the total absence of usage of defective features, but only to give an extra level of confidence that known problems have been avoided; they do not replace extensive testing and validation of the software.

7. RESULTS

The methodology presented in this paper has been applied to seven applications developed by Ansaldo-STS with the GNAT compiler, one using version 5.0.2 and six using version 6.1.1.

Version 5.0.2 had 201 KPRs. Out of these, 157 were classified as not safety critical. The 44 remaining ones could be tested with 36 checks (some checks were sufficient conditions for more than one KPR). 23 were fully automated checks, 8 required some extra manual inspection, and 5 required manual inspection of the build process (like checking that some compiler options were not used).

Version 6.1.1 had 140 KPRs. Out of these, 61 were classified as not safety critical. The 79 remaining ones could be tested with 41 checks. 37 were fully automated checks, 1 required some extra manual inspection, and 3 required manual inspection of the build process.

On a modest laptop (CPU at 1.73GHz, 512Mb RAM), running the verification process on 110 compilation units, 25634 raw SLOC took 1mn 32s. (wall-clock time). On a bigger application, 363 compilation units and 211251 raw SLOC, it took 13mn 11s.

Once the process was established, template documents prepared, etc., the effort for running the verification, inspecting the remaining cases manually, and producing the verification report was roughly one person-day. Note that this effort does not depend so much on the size of the project (running the tool is only a very small part of this time) than on the number of manual checks that remain. Note also that chasing a single bug that eventually appears to originate from a KPR can take much longer!

8. CONCLUSION

In this paper, we have shown how a static analysis tool (AdaControl in our experience) can be used to demonstrate that no feature corresponding to a known problem of a compiler is present in a piece of software.

Although this verification is required only by EN-50128 for railway systems, the methodology can be applied to any software where safety is a concern. The proposed methodology is based on the notion of *sufficient conditions*; it requires expertise for the analysis of the problem reports and the determination of the corresponding conditions, but the verification of the software can then be run casually by the developers as part of the normal development process.

The cost of applying the methodology proposed in this paper appears to be very low, compared to the overall effort spent in checking and certifying safety critical software. It shows that preventing software bugs by static analysis of KPRs can be very cost-effective.

9. ACKNOWLEDGEMENTS

Many thanks to the RAMS (*Reliability, Availability, Maintainability, Safety*) and SPP (*Standard Platform and Processes*) teams at Ansaldo-STS for many fruitful discussions regarding the proposed methodology and how it could fulfill the requirements of EN-50128.

10. REFERENCES

[1] ISO/IEC 15291:1999. Information technology — Programming languages — Ada Semantic Interface Specification (ASIS)

[2] EN-50128:2001. Railway applications. Communications, signalling and processing systems. Software for railway control and protection systems. ISBN 058037584 6

[3] AdaControl web site, http://www.adalog.fr/adacontrol2.htm

[4] "On the benefits for industrials of sponsoring free software development", *Ada User Journal*, Volume 26, n° 4, December 2005.

Wouldn't it be Nice to have Software Labels?

Organizer:
Elizabeth Fong
National Institute of Stds & Technology
Gaithersburg, MD, USA

Moderator:
Paul E. Black
National Institute of Stds & Technology
Gaithersburg, MD, USA

Panelists

Richard F. Leslie
SCORE

Simson Garfinkel
Naval Postgraduate School

Larry Wagoner
Department of Defense

Gary McGraw
Cigital

Jeff Williams
Aspect Security

Panel Topic

I can find out how much sodium is in a candy bar from the wrapper. New cars have an indication of their fuel efficiency, and Christmas lights have a UL tag. But how can a computer user gain insight into their software? Can the developer access this software remotely? Does it have copyrighted software that impairs my intellectual property if it is incorporated in my system? And from the developer side, what information could be furnished to communicate the quality of their work and products to acquirers? What information can help the software buyer decide which product is safer or most appropriate for their business?

This panel session will gather users and experts to discuss possible software label theory, delivery, and content, in addition to the benefits (and cautions) of having a software label. The goal of such a label is to present relevant information to empower consumers to make the right decisions. There is one possible model in the CESG Claims Tested Mark, and many proposals including Garfinkel's "Pure Software Act", and Lindstrom's software security data sheets. Some possible label criteria are that the software labeling and reporting are voluntary (not legislated), absolutely simple to produce, and content should be normalized across different scopes. Possible criteria for contents are that the facts are verifiable, objective, repeatable, and unambiguous.

Categories and Subject Descriptors

D.2.9 [Software Engineering Management]: Software Quality Assurance (SQA).

General Terms

Management, Documentation, Economics, Security, Standardization.

Keywords

Software facts, software labels, security data sheets, trustworthy system, transparency, provenance, pedigree.

PANELISTS VIEWPOINT

Richard F Leslie, SCORE, Counselors to America's Small Businesses

Small businesses face many challenges associated with assuring trustworthy software. Some of these may be mitigated with specific information on a "software label". The many small business owners who operate a very small office, store or home-based businesses rely on contractor services to provide information technology services, including information security. An easy-to-understand labeling system that is subject to testing and certification by an independent entity would serve the small business community well.

In addition to concerns about malicious acts, these business owners must also contend with normal wear and tear such as disk drive crashes or soda spills on the keyboard. The variety of problems is particularly an issue when there are only one, two or three people involved in a "virtual" business.

Any reliable rating system would bring peace of mind to ease one of the many dimensions that challenge small business owners in an ever more difficult business environment.

Larry Wagoner, Department of Defense

We are in the midst of tremendous changes in the way information flows to consumers. For example, on eBay, buyers rate sellers and so sellers nurture their "positive feedback" rating to keep their reputations intact. eBay would not have reached their level of success if there wasn't a label providing the reputation of a seller. Without such information, there wouldn't be any level of trust when one makes a purchase. Other sites use reviews and ratings of sellers. Another tremendous change underway is the increased information flowing to consumers via sites such as TripAdvisor. Pretty pictures with selective camera angles are no match for "real life" experiences reported by consumers. These and other models have changed the dynamics of information flow among buyers and sellers. For the most part, we lack this type of information flow in the software world.

There are two approaches open to information flow. First, stakeholders come to a consensus as to what should be reported and how. The FDA has done this for some types of medical devices. Alternatively we could allow information flow to be controlled for us. We could experience a regulation approach such as with food labels where the content is mandated, or we could see the emergence of consumer-oriented sites that provide the needed information. Either way, over time, buyers will increase their level of information.

Jeff Williams, Aspect Security

The software market is broken - at least as far as security is concerned. When security is invisible, buyers can't make informed decisions, and vendors have no incentive to create secure applications. Forcing vendors with liability and regulatory regimes encourages vendors to bury details about security and will not fix the market. This is why OWASP's mission is "to make application security visible, so that people and organizations can make informed decisions about true application security risks." We believe improved visibility will, over time, create a market for software that is not riddled with vulnerabilities. Even making simple facts visible can make a difference, such as whether the developers who built the software were trained in security, the security controls present in the software, the process used to build and test the software, etc... Currently, even the most basic facts are helpful, such as the languages used, the number of lines of code, libraries used, and connections made. This is not the time to let perfect be the enemy of good enough. We need software security labels now.

Simson Garfinkel, Naval Postgraduate School

Computer programs should not be given unrestricted access to the operating system. Instead, the specific capabilities that they require should be declared at the time of installation and then enforced by the operating system. These capabilities should be evidenced on a software "label" that should be visible both at the time of installation and through an auditing mechanism. This will allow users, computer security administrators, and consumer groups to easily audit software.

I proposed this approach back in 2003. Google has a similar system in it's Android platform.

Experience Report: Ada & Java Integration in the FAA's ERAM SWIM Program

Richard B. Schmidt
Lockheed Martin
Rockville, MD, USA
richard.b.schmidt@lmco.com

Abstract

The Ada language has been architected to provide a strong foundation for building software at the heart of safety critical, real-time, and long-maintained programs. The benefits of Ada in such environments have led to its use in a wide range of systems where correctness and predictability are critical. The current trend in our industry is to loosely tie systems together to share data that previously required manual re-entry, simply was not available, or worse could have been inconsistent between systems. This trend is resulting in a need to connect previously closed systems over in-house and external networks to perform that loose linkage.

The FAA has embraced this technology and has been developing an architecture, code framework, and standards for sharing data across their entire spectrum of Air Traffic Control systems and consumers. The FAA's overall umbrella for this is termed SWIM (System Wide Information Management), and programs participating in the architecture are called "SWIM implementing programs". The ERAM (EnRoute Automation Modernization) program I work on and previously presented at SIG Ada 2009 is one of the first SWIM implementing programs. ERAM has recently entered the test phase of the first increment of SWIM functionality. ERAM SWIM faced many of the same hurdles as other legacy Ada systems around the globe. The new interfaces are built on standard web protocols and need to provide secure reliable information flow to both other internal FAA systems, and external customers such as the major commercial air carriers.

In an effort to use best industry practices Lockheed Martin and the FAA chose Java and other web-standard technologies to implement much of the new SWIM interface. Java has gained a strong foothold in the internet environment and the classrooms for a variety of reasons. The result is that Java enjoys a large amount of FOSS and commercial support that makes it a natural choice for such a web interface, even in a high stakes environment such as ATC. ERAM SWIM development has encountered several issues with bridging the gap between Ada and Java and the quickly evolving world of FOSS/COTS SW.

Performance issues and command and control issues have dominated our internal discussions and been the focus of much of our effort to achieve test readiness. Efficient data representation, baseline control (remember much of it is FOSS), and debugging have also received a lot of attention. We had a lot of prior experience with mixed languages having several hundred thousand lines of C and C++ and considered ourselves prepared. However, integrating with Java is completely unlike integrating with those others, and we have had to adapt across the board to this new challenge. My talk will focus on the challenges we have encountered, and the lessons we have learned about the strengths and weaknesses of the various languages and other technology elements we have used implementing ERAM SWIM.

Categories and Subject Descriptors

D.3.0 PROGRAMMING LANGUAGES / General

General Terms

Management, Performance, Design, Reliability, Languages.

Keywords

Multi-Language Integration; Virtual Machine vs. Binding.

Bio

The speaker is a key software architect with the Lockheed Martin Information Systems & Global Services (IS&GS) - Civil group. The IS&GS - Civil group supports government projects including human space flight programs for NASA, biometric identification for the FBI, solutions to Transportation Security Administration and avionics/IT systems to the Department of Transportation. Lockheed Martin develops reliable, safety critical systems such as air traffic control systems that handle almost sixty percent of the world's air traffic. A Computer Science graduate from Virginia Polytechnic Institute and State University (Virginia Tech), Richard leads a group responsible for developing infrastructure and middleware solutions for the highly available, reliable, safety-critical ATC systems. In addition, Richard has a deep interest in reliable communications, full life-cycle problem determination, software fault-tolerance, automated testing, software reuse through proper abstraction and cross language applications.

"Unmanned Systems and Ada"

Industrial Presentation

Richard Weatherly, PhD

weather@mitre.org

703 983 7203

The MITRE Corporation

7525 Colshire Drive

McLean, VA 22102

ABSTRACT

The MITRE Corporation large ground robotic vehicle program relies on GNAT Ada running on the RTEMS open source operating system for all real-time, vehicle steering and propulsion control. This arrangement has worked satisfactorily for two years and has been the subject of SIGAda conference tutorials. Ada was selected for this application to address important safety and reliability concerns. The robotic vehicles weigh more than 1000 kg, can make zero-radius turns, and travel at 8 m/s. Such a vehicle could be dangerous if not properly managed. These Ada controlled, robotic vehicles are on display in the conference center parking lot. Please take a moment to see firsthand this application of Ada.

Categories and Subject Descriptors

D.1.3 Software [PROGRAMMING TECHNIQUES] Concurrent Programming: Parallel programming

General Terms: Languages, Reliability

Keywords: ada, autonomous systems, robotics.

Real-Time System Development in Ada using LEGO® Mindstorms® NXT

Peter J. Bradley
Real-Time Systems and Telematic
Services Architecture Group
Universidad Politécnica de Madrid
Madrid 28040, SPAIN

pbradley@datsi.fi.upm.es

Juan A. de la Puente
Real-Time Systems and Telematic
Services Architecture Group
Universidad Politécnica de Madrid
Madrid 28040, SPAIN

jpuente@dit.upm.es

Juan Zamorano
Real-Time Systems and Telematic
Services Architecture Group
Universidad Politécnica de Madrid
Madrid 28040, SPAIN

jzamora@datsi.fi.upm.es

ABSTRACT

In this paper, we describe a set of tools to fully develop a real-time application under Linux using as target the LEGO® Mindstorms® NXT robotics kit. These tools provide Real-Time & Embedded systems teachers with an alternative to conventional software models designed in classrooms and labs.

Categories and Subject Descriptors

K.3.2 [**Computers and Education**]: Computer and Information Science Education – *computer science education*.

C.3 [**Special-Purpose and Application-Based Systems**]: Real-Time and Embedded Systems.

D.3.2 [**Programming Languages**]: Language Classifications – *concurrent, distributed, and parallel languages*.

I.2.9 [**Artificial Intelligence**]: Robotics – *commercial robots and applications*.

General Terms: Design, Languages.

Keywords: Real-Time & Embedded systems education, Ada, Ravenscar, LEGO® Mindstorms®.

1. INTRODUCTION

The experience gained by students in real-time system development in classrooms and labs has been frequently reduced to software models which lack a "real" development experience. Economic and complexity drawbacks of physical devices have been outmatched in the past years with simple and flexible programmable robotics kits like LEGO® Mindstorms®.

Our purpose is to provide a set of tools, so that master students of Embedded & Real-Time Systems at the UPM are able to analyse, develop and implement a real-time system in Ada for LEGO® Mindstorms® robots complying with the Ravenscar profile [3].

This set of tools includes (see figure 1):

- A cross compilation system including compiler, assembler, linker, etc...
- An API to interact with LEGO® Mindstorms® peripherals

- A custom firmware for LEGO® Mindstorms®
- Communication tools between the target and the host to upload firmware and programs
- A remote debugging system or JTAG hardware debugging for LEGO® Mindstorms®
- A WCET tool to procure a timing analysis of the system
- A real-time modelling tool to evaluate the feasibility of the system

All of these tools will be running under Linux as most of them are available for Linux. Besides, it's the default OS used in our labs for software development.

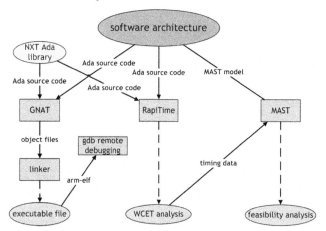

Figure 1. Development process.

2. TOOLS DESCRIPTION

The LEGO® Mindstorms® NXT [4] kit provides all the basic hardware features for classroom real-time system development. This is: an ARM7™ main processor, USB & bluetooth communications, I/O ports (motors, sensors …), and a considerable amount of LEGO® bricks to build complex models. Additionally, it offers support for a large variety of programming languages, which include Ada. There is a respectable and active research internet community.

Ada's concurrency and real-time integrated features as well as its hardware and interrupt handling support makes it the ideal choice for real-time system development.

The first step, once the physical device (LEGO® Mindstorms® NXT) and the programming language (Ada) have been established, is to build a cross compilation system hosted in Linux for an "arm-elf" target. AdaCore's GNAT GPL for LEGO® Mindstorms® 2009 [1] is hosted in Windows so a porting to Linux is needed. The packages to build include GNU Binutils (assembler, linker …), GMP & MPFR libraries (floating-point features), Newlib library (specific for embedded systems), gcc compiler and GNAT front end. The GNU build system (Autotools) is used throughout the building process.

The resulting compilation system uses the zero footprint runtime and has no tasking features. To provide tasking, the Ada API library supplied, relies on nxtOSEK [7] (OSEK [8] compliant system for LEGO® Mindstorms®). nxtOSEK depends on a modified LEGO® firmware (nxtBIOS or John Hansen's enhanced firmware [2]).

Once the cross compilation system is working on Linux, students are able to build their own real-time software for the LEGO® Mindstorms® using the Ada API. The way to upload software and firmware to the LEGO® Mindstorms® NXT from a Linux system is to use John Hansen's NeXTTool [2] or LibNXT [5].

In order to study the feasibility and scheduling aspects of the generated real-time application, a MAST model will by prepared by the students. MAST [6] is an open source set of tools, developed at Universidad de Cantabria, that enables modelling real-time applications and performing timing analysis of those applications. The MAST model can be used to represent real-time behaviour and requirements allowing an automatic schedulability analysis.

Figure 1 shows an overview of the development process.

3. SAMPLE APPLICATION

As proof of concept, a wired controlled vehicle will be designed, see figure 2. This vehicle has a front castor wheel used to turn and two back wheels, each with an independent motor. To control the vehicle we will use a wired joystick made up of a touch sensor to start/stop propulsion and a motor's encoder to control turns. Depending on the angle of the joystick encoder, different speed values will be send to the vehicle motors, thus turns are made possible, see figure 2.

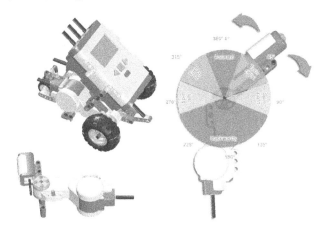

Figure 2. Wired controlled vehicle.

First, students must analyse the problem and come up with a software architecture. During this step, tasks, shared resources, events and relations between them, must be identified, see figure 3.

After, students must code the final design to Ada. Since a WCET tool hasn't yet been integrated, the physical model must be constructed in order to estimate the timing analysis of the system. This is done using the bluetooth API.

Finally, a MAST model is developed to study the feasibility and scheduling aspects of the vehicle project.

4. CONCLUSIONS & FUTURE WORK

We believe that a good foundation has been established for real-time & embedded system teachers to enlighten students in the

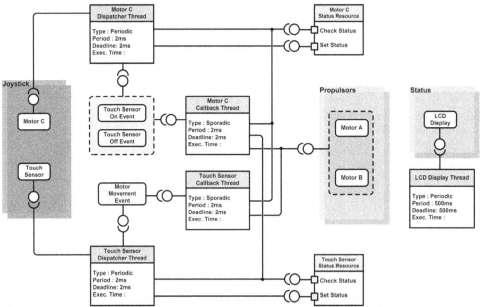

Figure 3. Software architecture.

development of "real" embedded platforms using Ada. The LEGO® Mindstorms® NXT kit offers all kinds of sensors and mechanisms to work with, even custom-made sensors can be developed. Also, there is a large and active internet community.

However, programming applications in Ada with the ZFP runtime, relying on nxtOSEK to achieve tasking and concurrency, is still far from ideal since no Ada tasking or protected objects features are accessible. Once AdaCore releases GNAT GPL for LEGO® Mindstorms® 2010 with Ravenscar runtime (due Sept. 2010) there will be no need to use nxtOSEK and all Ada features that comply with the Ravenscar profile will be operative. As with the 2009 version, a Linux port will be made accessible from our web page[1].

Future work could adapt a WCET tool like RapiTime [10] or Bound-T [9] to our development process. Remote debugging could be achieved using a TCP based communication between LEGO® Mindstorms® and gdb via USB connection. Alternatively, hardware debugging using JTAG is also possible.

---

[1] http://polaris.dit.upm.es/~str/index.html

5. REFERENCES

[1] Ada-Core Technologies, The GNAT Pro Company. http://www.adacore.com/

[2] Bricx Command Center. http://bricxcc.sourceforge.net/

[3] Burns, A., 1999. *The Ravenscar Profile*. ACM SIGADA Ada Letters, 19(4):49–52.

[4] LEGO® MINDSTORMS® Hardware Developer Kit (HDK), 2006. http://mindstorms.lego.com, LEGO Group.

[5] LibNXT, NXT host control library. http://code.google.com/p/libnxt/

[6] MAST - Modeling and Analysis Suite for Real-Time Applications, Universidad de Cantabria. http://mast.unican.es/

[7] nxtOSEK Project. Takashi Chikamasa, 2007. http://lejos-osek.sourceforge.net/

[8] OSEK/VDX - Operating System, version 2.2.3, February 2005. http://portal.osek-vdx.org/files/pdf/specs/os223.pdf

[9] Peterson, S., 2005. *Porting the Bound-T WCET tool to Lego Mindstorms and the Asterix RTOS*. Master's thesis. Mälardalen University, Västerås,Sweden.

[10] Rapita Systems LTD. http://www.rapitasystems.com/

Parallelism Generics for Ada 2005 and Beyond

Brad J. Moore
General Dynamics Canada
1020 68th Ave. N.E., Calgary, Alberta, Canada
001.403.730.1367

Brad.moore@gdcanada.com

ABSTRACT

The Ada programming language is seemingly well-positioned to take advantage of emerging multi-core technologies. While it has always been possible to write parallel algorithms in Ada, there are certain classes of problems however, where the level of effort to write parallel algorithms outweighs the ease and simplicity of a sequential approach. This can result in lost opportunities for parallelism and slower running software programs. Languages such as Cilk++[1] and OpenMB provide expressive mechanisms to add parallelism to code using a C++ based syntax by adding special syntactic directives where parallelism is desired. This paper explores Ada's concurrency features to see whether it is possible to easily inject similar iterative and recursive parallelism to code written in Ada, without having to resort to special language extensions or non-standard language features. This paper identifies a "work-seeking" technique, which can be viewed as a form of compromise between work-sharing and work-stealing, two other existing strategies. The paper presents performance results to illustrate the benefits of use for the generics and goes on to suggest how parallelism pragmas could possibly be added to the Ada programming language to further facilitate writing parallel applications.

Categories and Subject Descriptors

D.1.3 [**Programming Techniques**]: Concurrent Programming – *parallel programming*; D.3.3 [**Programming Languages**]: Language Constructs and Features – *concurrent programming structures, data types and structures, recursion.*; D.2.13 [**Software Engineering**]: Reusable Software – *reusable libraries*; F.1.2 [**Computation by Abstract Devices**]: Modes of Computation – *parallelism and concurrency*; F.1.2 [**Computation by Abstract Devices**]: Studies of Program Constructs – *program and recursion schemes*; G.1.0 [**Mathematics of Computing**]: Numerical Analysis – *parallel algorithms*.

General Terms

Algorithms, Performance, Design, Reliability, Standardization, Languages.

Keywords

Ada 2005, Work-Seeking, Work-Stealing, Work-Sharing, multi-core, hyper-threads.

1. INTRODUCTION

Computers with multi-core processors are now entry level choices in the consumer marketplace. The general trend for increasing numbers of cores brings new opportunities for parallelism in applications. The Ada programming language already provides a solid framework for concurrency and parallelism as it is the only ISO standard object-oriented, concurrent, real-time programming language[2]. Ada has supported concurrency since its inception, and each revision of the language has improved Ada's concurrency offerings[3]. In this paper, a suite of Ada generics are described that may be applied to iterative loops and nested recursions to take better advantage of multi-core hardware in order to reduce processing times.

2. ITERATIVE PARALLELISM

Consider if one were asked to write some code to produce the sum of all integers between 1 and a million. The sequential version of this code is straightforward and easy to write;

```
Sum : Integer := 0;
for I in 1 .. 1_000_000 loop
   Sum := Sum + I;
end loop;
```

If the code is to be run on a target with multi-core processors and optimal performance is a goal, it might be reasonable to attempt restructuring of the code to execute the loop in parallel.

At first glance, it appears that a simple divide and conquer strategy is needed whereby the iterations are divided amongst available processors. When one attempts to convert this code to take advantage of multiple processors however, several obstacles are encountered.

1. The number of processors may not be known statically. For example, it is desirable that code intended to run on generic desktops should determine the number of available processors and then divide the iterations evenly between available processors. Ideally, distributed overhead should be minimal such that the code is able to run as fast on a machine with a single processor as the sequential code snippet above.

2. Race conditions are a problem if the loop refers to variables declared in an enclosing scope. For example, care must be taken to ensure that the variable **Sum** does not get corrupted by concurrent updates from multiple tasks. Some sort of synchronization is needed to prevent these sorts of problems, yet synchronizing on each iteration through the loop introduces overhead and forces the code to run more sequentially, defeating the purpose of attempting a parallel approach.

3. A parallel approach can quickly become complex and error prone. Tasks need to be defined and created. The iteration range needs to be divided up between the number of available processors, accounting for such possibilities as when the number of processors does not divide evenly into the number of iterations. This extra complexity can be hard to justify whenever programmers need to use iterative and recursive constructs.

For example, assuming a processor with dual cores, one might write;

```
function Parallel_Addition_Manual
      return Integer is

   task type Worker is
      entry Initialize
       (Start_Index,
        Finish_Index : Integer);
      entry Total (Result : out Integer);
   end Worker;

   task body Worker is
      Start, Finish : Integer;
      Sum : Integer := 0;
   begin
      accept Initialize
       (Start_Index, Finish_Index : Integer)
      do
         Start := Start_Index;
         Finish := Finish_Index;
      end Initialize;

      for I in Start .. Finish loop
         Sum := Sum + I;
      end loop;
```

```
      accept Total (Result : out Integer) do
         Result := Sum;
      end Total;
   end Worker;


   Number_Of_Processors : constant := 2;
   Workers : array (1 .. Number_Of_Processors)
      of Worker;


   Results : array (1 .. Number_Of_Processors)
      of Integer;
begin -- Parallel_Addition_Manual
   Workers (1).Initialize (1, 500_000);
   Workers (2).Initialize
      (500_001, 1_000_000);
   Workers (1).Total (Results (1));
   Workers (2).Total (Results (2));


   return Results (1) + Results (2);
end Parallel_Addition_Manual;
```

This code assumes that there are two processors available. Generalizing the code to run on any number of processors adds further complexity to the code. In any case, it is evident that the amount of code needed to manually add parallelism on a case by case basis may be hard to justify for simple loops.

This paper describes a set of reusable components that can be used to inject parallelism into code in order to speed up processing for loops, recursive data structures and recursive algorithms.

3. THE APPROACH

Ideally, we would like to see capabilities that:

1. Provide parallelism while minimizing visible differences from the sequential version of the code.

2. Allow the injected parallelism to be at the site of the sequential version of the loop or recursive construct. A potential solution should not require relocating the loop code outside the enclosing subprogram, since that could involve significant code restructuring.

3. Provide support for adding parallelism to loops, but also facilitate adding parallelism to other constructs such as recursive data structures and other forms of recursive algorithms.

4. The parallelism should maintain the sequential order of operations used to create the result. For example, the following loop should produce the same result as if the code were executed sequentially. The nodes in the resulting linked list should contain the same values in the same order.

```ada
package Integer_List is new

    Ada.Containers.Doubly_Linked_Lists

        (Integer);

Data : Integer_List.List;

for I in 1 .. 100 loop

    Data.Append (I);

end loop;
```

4.   THE SOLUTION

The strategy to add parallelism to iterative loops is a divide and conquer strategy whereby the total range of iterations are "split" into smaller sub-ranges managed by separate worker tasks that are scheduled to run on different processors.

If a result of a global scope is to be generated by the iteration, then a local copy of the result variable is given to every task. As each worker task completes its work, the local result is merged into the final global result using a reducing operation. This operation is called reduction because the multiple results of each worker are reduced to a single value.

This initial approach can be considered to be a simple form of Work-Sharing. Work-Sharing is generally describes as a strategy where work is divided between members of a team[4].

For this to work and maintain the same ordering for the combination of results as if the result were generated sequentially, the reducing operation needs to be an associative operation. Examples of associative operations include addition, determining min/max, and appending items to a list. Multiplication of floating point is technically not an associative operation due to rounding errors, though the result of the operation may be considered to be accurate enough to be treated as though it were associative.

For a target platform with two processors, creating the sum of integers from 1 to 1,000,000 could involve two worker tasks executing the code. One worker could be tasked with iterating from 1 .. 500,000, and the other worker could be assigned to iterate from 500,001 .. 1,000,000. To avoid race conditions, each worker task is given its own copy of the global result variable referenced in the loop. (In this case, both tasks would have their own Sum variable.) Each task would need to initialize its copy of the global variable to a starting value, called the identity value.

When the two worker tasks complete, the results of both worker tasks need to be combined (reduced). In this case, the reduction operation involves simply adding the results together. The reduction operation for a procedure that populates a linked list might involve appending the linked list result of one worker to another workers partial linked list result.

In general, the data type being operated on needs to have the properties of a monoid. A monoid is a concept from the field of abstract algebra that includes an associative binary operation and an identity element. The identity element has the property that when applied to the object using the associative binary operation it results in the same value. A binary operation is associative if the operation can be applied in any order within an expression without impacting the final result. e.g., $(A + B) + C = A + (B + C)$

For example, for integers, if the associative binary operation is addition, then the identity element is 0. If the associative binary operation is multiplication, then the identity element is 1. For a linked list, if the associative binary operation is appending, then the identity element is an empty list.

Adding parallelism to a loop with a known number of iterations, such as a for loop, involves enclosing the loop in a procedure that provides the bounds of the iteration, and then enclosing the procedure in a declaration block that calls an instantiation of a generic that manages the parallelism.

If we reconsider the following sequential code;

```ada
declare

    Sum : Integer := 0;

begin

    for I in 1 .. 1_000_000 loop

        Sum := Sum + I;

    end loop;

end;
```

The work-sharing parallel version of this code might look like;

```ada
with Integer_Addition_Reducer;

declare

    Final_Sum : Integer := 0;

    procedure Iteration

            (Start, Finish : Positive;

            Sum : in out Integer) is

    begin

        for I in Start .. Finish loop

            Sum := Sum + I;

        end loop;

    end Iteration;

begin

    Integer_Addition_Reducer

        (From => 1,

        To => 1_000_000,

        Process => Iteration'Access,

        Item => Final_Sum);

end;
```

This solution uses a feature of Ada that is not present in many of the other mainstream languages. Most languages have some form of nesting support, but Ada carries this further and allows procedures to be nested within declarative blocks. This is an important part of this solution, because it allows the looping logic to remain at the site of the sequential loop. Having to move the sequential logic to a procedure outside the scope from where the sequential form of the loop would normally reside can lead to significant restructuring of the code, particularly if global results are not visible at the site of new location.

The Integer_Addition_Reducer call is a reuseable instantiation of a generic procedure.

```
with Parallel.Iterate_And_Reduce;

procedure Integer_Addition_Reducer is

    new Parallel.Iterate_And_Reduce

      (Iteration_Index_Type => Positive,

       Element_Type => Integer,

       Reducer => "+",

       Identity_Value => 0);
```

where Iteration_Index_Type is the data type of the loop iterator variable, Element_Type is the monoid result type, Reducer is the associative reducing operation of the monoid, and Identity_Value is the identity element of the monoid.

Parallel.Iterate_And_Reduce is the generic procedure that manages the parallelism. The generic Reducer formal parameter satisfies the following call profile;

```
function Reducer

       (Left, Right : Element_Type)

            return Element_Type;
```

All parallel iterative and recursive generics are generic subprograms that are child subprograms of package Parallel, which provides some shared type declarations.

Most notably, the Work_Seeking_State type is defined. This type is used to represent the Boolean value that is shared between the worker tasks to indicate that idle workers are seeking work. It is important that this type is declared atomic, since multiple tasks can update the Boolean without synchronization. The synchronization, when necessary, is managed by a protected type within the implementation of the generic.

```
    type Work_Seeking_State is

       record

          Seeking_Work : Boolean;

       end record;

    pragma Atomic (Work_Seeking_State);
```

5.   WORK-SEEKING VERSION

A loop iteration typically takes the same amount of time as subsequent iterations through the same loop. Even when there are differences, so long as these differences are distributed randomly across the range of iterations, a simple divide and conquer approach should provide optimal parallelism. However, there are certain classes of loops where these properties do not hold true.

For example, the amount of processing may increase for each subsequent iteration. For these sorts of loops, a simple divide and conquer strategy may be suboptimal, as it may be beneficial to incorporate some form of load-balancing. Ideally, if a worker task allocated to a processor completes before other worker tasks, the

worker on the idle processor would arrange to take work from other workers to further divide up the remaining work.

One approach in the literature is called work-stealing where the idle worker task attempts to steal work from other workers typically by searching randomly through the other busy worker tasks looking for more work.

Another approach known as work-sharing often involves placing the work items in a centralized queue, and as each worker completes its task, the next work item is extracted from the centralized queue and given to the idle worker.

This paper identifies a third approach that can be seen as a compromise between work-sharing and work-stealing. The idle task does not "steal" work from other tasks, but instead issues a "request" for work (i.e., seeks work). Busy worker tasks perform a simple check of an atomic Boolean shared between all the worker tasks during each iteration to see if there are any idle workers looking for work.

If the Boolean flag is set and the busy worker has extra work to offer, then the busy worker task clears the Boolean flag and then makes a work "offer" through a protected object by offering half of its remaining iteration range. If the offer is accepted by an idle worker, then both workers continue with their newly assigned iteration subranges. If the offer is not accepted, (as would be the case if another worker task also noticed the work request and made an earlier offer), then the offering task continues on with its original set of remaining iterations. If the Boolean flag is not set when it is checked during an iteration, then the worker completes its iteration and proceeds to the next iteration.

Introducing work-seeking capabilities into the programmers sequential code involves making some relatively minor changes to the looping as described for the work-sharing case. Specifically, an atomic Boolean parameter is declared just before the procedure enclosing the loop that indicates whether there are idle tasks requesting work. This is an aliased Boolean, so that the management of the Boolean can be handled by the generic procedure, which gains access to the Boolean via a passed access parameter.

In addition, to take advantage of work-seeking, the loop requires adding the Boolean check, and the loop end parameter must be converted to an in out parameter so that the loop can indicate how much work has already been done. The previous example converted to a work-seeking version now becomes;

```
with Work_Seeking_Integer_Addition_Reducer;

...

declare

    Sum : Integer := 0;

    Other_Workers : aliased
       Parallel.Work_Seeking_State;

    procedure Iteration
       (Start : Integer;
        Finish : in out Integer;
        Sum : in out Integer) is

    begin
```

```ada
      for I in Start .. Finish loop
         Sum := Sum + I;
         if Other_Workers.Seeking_Work then
            Other_Workers.Seeking_Work :=
               (Seeking_Work => False);
            Finish := I;
            exit;
         end if;
      end loop;
   end Iteration;
begin

   Work_Seeking_Integer_Addition_Reducer
      (From => 1,
       To => 1_000_000,
       Process => Iteration'Access,
       Other_Workers => Other_Workers'Access
       Item => Sum);

end;
```

The work-seeking version adds the distributed overhead of a Boolean check in the working task per iteration, which can be offset by gains in parallelism. It is interesting to note however, that testing has shown that the Boolean check can be removed from the loop, causing the work-seeking version to degenerate to the work-sharing case and the work-seeking version of the generic will execute at speeds comparable to the work-sharing instance of the generic.

A work-stealing approach was considered whereby the work stealer would randomly select busy workers, suspend the worker, then steal work, but this approach was disregarded because in order to eliminate distributed overhead on the busy worker, the work stealer would need to suspend the busy worker. Ada provides mechanisms to do this, using the features of the package Ada.Asynchronous_Task_Control, however this package is not usually implemented on platforms involving a general purpose OS, because most operating systems do not currently provide support for suspending other threads, for various reasons. Because of this, the Work-Seeking approach was seen as a reasonable alternative that is generally available for use.

Note also that Work-Stealing typically would involve the idle worker randomly searching busy workers looking for work to steal, whereas with work-seeking, there is a cooperative hand-off between the busy worker and the idle worker. This eliminates the need for the random searching and could offset some of gains that might be realized through work-stealing. Further note that the distributed overhead of a Boolean check may not be significant compared to the main loop logic, and choosing between the performance differences of work-seeking and work-stealing may be a case of diminishing returns.

6. RECURSIVE PARALLELISM

The previous examples show generics that add parallelism to iterative loops. A similar approach can be applied to add parallelism to recursive code. While the general concept of dividing the work equally between processors applies, there are some different constraints. With iterative parallelism, the number of iterations is known up front before entering the loop, and calculations can be applied to divide the work. With recursion, the total number of iterations is not as relevant, because the work cannot generally be divided based on the number of iterations.

Instead, the strategy is to split the work as soon as possible during the recursion, so that different branches of recursion can be assigned to different processors.

With recursion, it is important to know how many branches exist at each level of recursion. An attempt is made to divide the number of processors evenly between each branch of the recursion. This division is reapplied at each level of recursion with the assigned subset of processors, until the number of processors associated with a recursive branch is one.

Consider if one were asked to write some code to calculate the Fibonacci sequence in parallel. The Fibonacci value for an integer X can be expressed recursively as;

$$Fibonacci (X) = Fibonacci (X – 2) + Fibonacci (X – 1)$$

The sequential form of this algorithm can be expressed in Ada as;

```ada
function Fibonacci (Value : Natural)
   return Natural is
begin
   if Value < 2 then
      return Value;
   else
      return Fibonacci (Value - 2) +
             Fibonacci (Value - 1);
   end if;
end Fibonacci;
```

Assuming dual cores, and that a work-sharing strategy is desired, the strategy would be to assign the initial calculation of Fibonacci (Value – 2) to one core, and the calculation of Fibonacci (Value – 1) to the other core. Once the call has recursed to a level where all workers are busy, the remaining recursion is processed sequentially without further attempts to divide work between processors.

This work-sharing approach requires that two versions of the processing are provided to the generic. One version is the sequential version, and the second is a parallel version where instead of calling itself recursively, a call is made to an access-to-subprogram variable set by the generic that manages the recursion. The generic starts off by calling the parallel version, and the initial worker is associated with a value representing the total number of subordinate workers that the worker should employ when parallelism opportunities are encountered. This number is divided between each of the subordinate branches of recursion, as evenly as possible. The rightmost subordinate branch of each recursion is assumed to be work assigned to the parent branch, so there is no actual hand-off in this case. This worker count continues to be subdivided at each level of recursion in a similar fashion until subordinate workers are given a value of one. When this count becomes one for a specific worker, that worker is no longer responsible for handing off work to subordinate workers, and then the processing switches over to the sequential recursion routine for the remaining work for that branch.

Whenever work is handed off to a subordinate and a reduction result is needed, an entry is created in a special bounded linked list data structure that will store the result for that worker. The result node in the linked list is inserted to the right or left of the parent worker, depending on whether the new worker is considered to be to the right or left of the parent worker based on the recursive structure. When a parallel hand-off occurs, the parent worker assumes the result returned for the subordinate branch is the monoid identity value, and then proceeds to process its other branches of recursion.

When a worker completes its recursion, it first reduces its result into its slot in the reduction list, which may already have a value from completed worker nodes to the right of the worker. If the worker's node is not the leftmost node, the worker then reduces the resulting node value into the worker node to the left, and then removes itself from the linked list structure. Once all work is complete for all workers, there should be only one node remaining in the reduction list, which is the original leftmost node, which contains the final result value.

The reducing link list data structure is a bounded protected object that utilizes entry families to minimize contention on the link list. The data structure was influenced by an elegant solution to the Dining Philosophers problem [5]. The Reducing Linked List is similar except the philosophers chopsticks are represented by nodes in the link list and the Philosophers are represented by Workers, and instead of a circular table, the philosophers are organized in a row, based on their position in the linked list.

It should be noted that none of the parallelism generics involve heap allocation. All storage is stack based, and bounded based on the number of workers prescribed for the task.

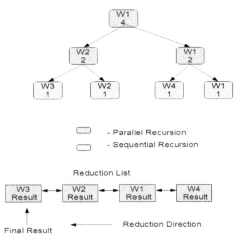

Figure 1 - Recursive Approach for four cores

Using the parallel generics for recursive parallelism, the code for parallel Fibonacci becomes;

```ada
with Parallel.Elementary_Reducing_Recurse;
use Parallel;

function Fibonacci (Value : Natural)

    return Natural

is

    type Recursion_Routine is access
        function
            (Number : Natural;
             Direction :
                 Parallel.Recursion_Direction;
             Split :
                 Parallel.Positive_Worker_Count;
             Of_Splits :
                 Parallel.Positive_Worker_Count)
        return Natural;


    -- Set by call to
    --    Two_Way_Recursive_Integer_Addition
    Recurse : aliased Recursion_Routine
      := null;


    function Parallel_Fibonacci
        (Number : Natural) return Natural
    is
    begin
        if Number < 2 then
            return Number;
        else

            return
              Recurse
                (Number => Number - 1,
                 Direction  => Left,
                 Split => 1,
                 Of_Splits => 2)
              +
              Recurse
                (Number => Number - 2,
                 Direction => Right,
                 Split => 2,
                 Of_Splits => 2);

        end if;
```

46

```
end Parallel_Fibonacci;

function Sequential_Fibonacci
   (Number : Natural) return Natural is
begin
   if Number < 2 then
      return Number;
   else
      return
         Sequential_Fibonacci(Number - 2)
          +
         Sequential_Fibonacci(Number - 1);
   end if;
end Sequential_Fibonacci;

function
   Two_Way_Recursive_Integer_Addition
is new Parallel.
   Elementary_Reducing_Recurse
      (Work_Type => Natural,
       Result_Type => Natural,
       Reducer => "+",
       Identity_Value => 0,
       Recursion_Routine =>
          Recursion_Routine);
begin -- Fibonacci
   return Two_Way_Recursive_Integer_Addition
      (Item  => Value,
       Recursion => Recurse'Access,
       Parallel_Process =>
          Parallel_Fibonacci'Access,
       Sequential_Process =>
          Sequential_Fibonacci'Access);
end Fibonacci;
```

7.   WORK SEEKING VERSION

A transformation similar to that needed for work-seeking iteration is needed to get work-seeking applied to parallel recursion. When workers complete their work, they request more work. A busy worker checks an atomic Boolean flag at each level of recursion to see if other workers are seeking work. If so, then the parent worker may offer work in the form of a subordinate branch of recursion to the idle worker. As with all the previously described reducing generics, this results in a node being reinserted into the reduction list that represents the idle worker. As before, the new node is inserted to the right or left of the offerer, depending on whether the work being assigned is considered to belong to the left or right of the

parent node. Note the similarity between the work-sharing version, as well as the similarities between the work-sharing iterative version vs. the work-seeking iterative version. In this case, there is only one subprogram that needs to be passed to the generic. The parallel and sequential code both exist, but are contained within the single procedure, and the Boolean flag is used to distinguish between parallel and sequential recursion.

```
with Parallel.
   Elementary_Work_Seeking_Reducing_Recurse;
use Parallel;

function Fibonacci (Value : Natural)
   return Natural
is
   Other_Workers : aliased
      Parallel.Work_Seeking_State;

   type Recursion_Routine is access function
      (Number : Natural;
       Direction :
          Parallel.Recursion_Direction;
       Split :
          Parallel.Positive_Worker_Count;
       Of_Splits :
          Parallel.Positive_Worker_Count)
             return Natural;

   -- Set by call to
   --    Two_Way_Recursive_Integer_Addition
   Recurse : aliased Recursion_Routine
      := null;

   function Parallel_Fibonacci
      (Number : Natural) return Natural is
   begin
      if Number < 2 then
         return Number;
      elsif not Other_Workers.Seeking_Work
      then
         return
            Parallel_Fibonacci (Number - 2)
             +
            Parallel_Fibonacci (Number - 1);
      else
         return
            Recurse
```

```ada
         (Number => Number - 1,
          Direction  => Left,
          Split => 1,
          Of_Splits => 2)
        +
        Recurse
          (Number => Number - 2,
           Direction => Right,
           Split => 2,
           Of_Splits => 2);
    end if;
  end Parallel_Fibonacci;


  function
     Two_Way_Recursive_Integer_Addition
  is new Parallel.
   Elementary_Work_Seeking_Reducing_Recurse
     (Work_Type => Natural,
      Result_Type => Natural,
      Reducer => "+",
      Identity_Value => 0,
      Recursion_Routine =>
        Recursion_Routine);
begin
  return Two_Way_Recursive_Integer_Addition
    (Item   => Value,
     Other_Workers => Other_Workers'Access,
     Recursion => Recurse'Access,
     Process => Parallel_Fibonacci'Access);
end Fibonacci;
```

8.   NOW AND BEYOND ADA 2012

The parallelism generics described previously enable programmers to add parallelism more easily to their code. If this capability is seen as being useful, then perhaps some syntactic sugar could be added to the language to further simplify readability of the code.

Supposing that special pragmas could be specified for iterative loops and recursive subprograms. Ideally these pragmas would be as simple as possible to use, but it is unlikely that a compiler would be able to easily determine the reducing functions, identity values, and global variables without some sort of indication from the programmer.

Also, it may be desirable if most of this code can be treated as being the facilities of a generic Ada package rather than entirely magic provided by the compiler. There would still need to be some magic involved, but this would mostly be in the form of "glue" code to transform the sequential construct into the parallel form invoking the generic instance.

The Parallel parent package could itself be a child of Ada (Ada.Parallel), and generic child packages of Ada.Parallel could be treated specially such that the compiler could extract the reducing function, reduction type, and identity value from the instance of the generic, as well determine which transformation is needed based on which generic package is used to create the instance.

With this approach, the programmer provides all the information needed by the compiler by specifying the name of the generic instance to be applied. If the pragma is ignored by the compiler, then the code runs sequentially, as though the pragma did not exist.

The form for the iterative loop pragma could be;

pragma Parallel_Loop ({Using =>} Parallel_Instance_Name);

and a similar pragma for recursive subprograms might be;

pragma Parallel_Subprogram
        ({Using =>} Parallel_Instance_Name);

Then it might be possible to write the previous iterative example as;

```ada
with Iterative_Integer_Sum;
...
Sum : Integer := 0;
for I in 1 .. 100_000_000 loop
   Sum := Sum + I;
end loop;
pragma Parallel_Loop
 (Using => Iterative_Integer_Sum);
```

The idea is that the compiler would transform this code into the code shown in the corresponding previous example, and that the compiler could provide safety by ensuring that the loop would only contain write references to a single variable of global scope, and only if the type of the global variable matches the reduction type of the instance. If the named instance did not have associated reduction results, then no global write references would be allowed within the loop. There could be an exception to these rules to allow write references, if the reference is an array reference using the iteration index. This could be allowed, but only if a single index value is used to reference the array within each iteration. Otherwise, the code likely has dependencies on values generated by other iterations which is not suitable for transformation into parallel code.

Similarly, for the previous recursive parallelism example, one might be able to write;

```ada
with Recursive_Natural_Sum;

function Fibonacci (Value : Natural)
    return Natural is
begin
   if Value < 2 then
      return Value;
```

```
    else

      return Fibonacci (Value - 2) +
              Fibonacci (Value - 1);

    end if;

end Fibonacci;
```

pragma Parallel_Subprogram
(Using => Recursive_Natural_Sum);

These syntactic suggestions are only ideas that may or may not withstand closer scrutiny. In any case, it is too late to consider such changes for the forthcoming Ada 2012 amendment to the language, however these ideas may be worth considering for a subsequent language amendment if the feature is easy enough to implement, and there is sufficient interest for adding further parallelism support to Ada.

In the meantime, it should be possible to develop a preprocessor utility that provides this capability today. Such a preprocessor would quickly scan the Ada source text for the existence of Parallel_Loop pragmas and Parallel_Subprogram pragmas. If such pragmas are detected, then a utility using the Ada Semantic Interface Specification (ASIS)[6] could be invoked to apply the needed transformation of the Ada source code from the sequential construct to the parallel form. Such a utility could also perform various checks to help ensure that the sequential construct can be safely transformed into a parallel construct. If checks fail, then the compilation would be aborted and would result in the reporting of an appropriate error message. If the transformation completes successfully, the reconstructed Ada source code would be output as an intermediate source file that is then passed to the compiler for compilation, as legal Ada 2005 source.

It should be possible to integrate such a preprocessor into a development environment without too much difficulty. For instance, the GNAT compiler already provides support for preprocessing using the gnatprep utility. The configurability of the GPS IDE and the GNAT build environment should provide enough flexibility to integrate another preprocessor. If there is enough interest and the ideas are worth implementing, then perhaps compiler vendors could consider adding experimental support in some form or other. Compiler vendors tend to be motivated by customer requests, if the requests are reasonable.

9.   TEST RESULTS

The generics created thus far can be classified as supporting iterative (looping) parallelism, or recursive parallelism. The generics can be further classified by whether a reduction result is produced or not. Each generic has a work-seeking and a work-sharing form, and reducing forms exist for elementary types (function return results) and composite types (procedure in out parameters)

Test programs have been written for manipulating linked lists, solving linear algebra matrices, implementing a binary tree recursive container, creating Bernoulli sequences using Big Number libraries, determining if a number is a prime number, embarrassingly parallel problems[7] such as solving partial differential equations and so on. Testing has shown favorable results on both Windows and Linux operating systems.

The following test results were collected using an ASUS notebook running Windows 7 on an Intel Atom 333 1.6 Ghz CPU which features dual cores with 4 threads. The code was compiled using the Adacore GNAT GPL 2010 version of the compiler. No optimization was used in the compiler switches for the project, however the Suppress_All_Checks flag was enabled. Many different settings were tried, and it was found that the two settings that influenced the speed most noticeably were the optimization setting, and the Suppress_All_Checks setting. Running without suppressing the checks only slows the code down somewhat, but still results in timely results.

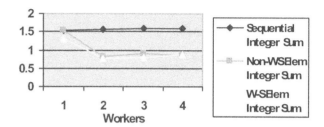

Figure 2 - Elemenary Integer Sum

This test involved calculating the sum of all integers between 1 and 400 million. In this case, an almost equivalent increase in speed was seen between one and two workers. The sequential version in the test is a simple loop without any of the generic code, so it is worth noting that even with one worker, both generic forms run as well or better than the simple sequential form. The Work Seeking version performed marginally better overall, which is somewhat surprising because this problem is one that involves a problem where the work load is evenly balanced at program startup. Adding additional workers beyond 2 did not provide any benefits in execution time.

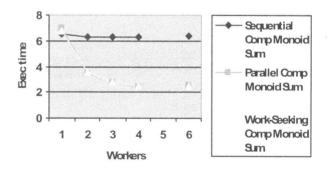

Figure 3 - Composite (Tagged Type) Sum

This test similarly involved calculating the sum of all integers between 1 and 400 million, except that instead of applying to integer, a composite tagged type structure was used that contained an integer component. The Composite forms of the generics were used. In this case, an almost linear increase was seen between one and two workers, but additional performance was seen up to the number of hyper-threads associated with the processor (four). Otherwise, the results are similar to the previous test, except slower, likely due to the increase in the size of the data type. Also, the work-seeking and work-sharing versions of the code are almost indistinguishable.

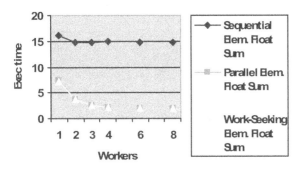

Figure 4 - Elementary Float Sum

This test is similar to the previous tests, except that floating point values were used instead of integers. Some rather interesting results were seen here. In particular, for a single worker, the generic code significantly outperformed the sequential version of the code. The reason for this difference is unknown. It may have something to do with the generics triggering the code to run at higher CPU speeds, or perhaps better use of system caches. In any case, it seems that the parallelism generics seem to provide significant advantage for floating point calculations. The generics also were run on an Intel i7 processor (not shown here), and similar improvements were seen up to the number of available hyper-threads (Eight). The improvement on this processor was noticeably more linear than for integer calculations. As before, the work-seeking generic performs comparably with the work-sharing generic.

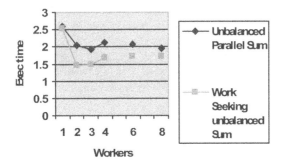

Figure 5 - Unbalanced Iteration (Elementary Integer Sum)

This test attempts to provide an example that shows the benefits of iterative work-seeking. In this case, each iteration through the loop involved performing more calculations than the previous iteration. The workers on the lower range of the iteration should complete much earlier than those processing the higher range of iterations. The results were not as dramatic as expected, but they do show that the work-seeking version has noticeably better execution times. The performance seems to deteriorate once the number of worker is increased above the number of available cores (two).

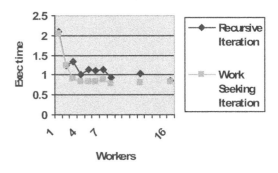

Figure 6 - Recursive Iteration

This test involves a special binary tree generic container that was written to use the recursive parallelism generics. The element type in this case, is the containers node data type. The container implements a red-black tree structure which is not a perfectly balanced tree[8]. It is a left leaning tree, in that a significantly higher number of nodes will always be found on the left side of the tree. This describes a scenario where we would expect work-seeking to provide benefits over work-sharing. This test does not involve any reduction, and simply involves iterating over all the nodes stored in the container, and applying a client specified Process subprogram similar to the Iterate subprogram of the Ada.Containers.Doubly_Linked_List generic. Indeed, the test results show that work-seeking provides a more consistent result with better performance. The improvement seems to level off once the number of workers equals the number of available hyper-threads.

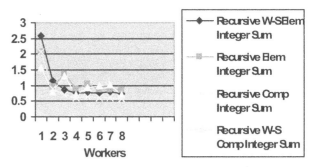

Figure 7 - Recursive Integer Reduction

This test involves the same binary tree generic container used in the previous example, except special reducing generics of the container are used to generate a single result from iterating through all the nodes. In this case, both elementary and composite reduction routines were used. As before, the work-seeking versions seem to provide more consistent results that outperformed the work-sharing versions. It is interesting to note that the composite routines seemed to outperform the elementary form, even though the reduction result type happended to be an elementary type (Integer).

In this case, it appears that passing integer results as in out parameters is slightly more efficient than returning as function results, though further testing would be needed to determine if this actually is the case. As before, the performance levels off once the number of workers reaches the number of available hyper-threads.

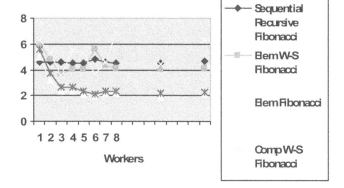

Figure 8 - Recursive Fibonacci

This test involves applying the recursive generics to a recursive algorithm (the Fibonacci example described earlier), instead of a recursive data structure. The work load for this problem is unbalanced because the amount of recursion needed to calculate the Fibonacci value for N – 2 can be significantly less than the amount of recursion needed to calculate the Fibonacci value for N – 1. One would expect that a work-seeking approach would outperform a work-sharing approach. The results obtained however were very much the opposite of what was expected. Where Work-Sharing previously provided inconsistent results, consistent results were obtained. The work-sharing consistently outperformed the work-seeking version by a noticeable margin. A possible explanation for these results is not forthcoming. Further investigation will be needed, however these results do show that results can be surprising, and it may not be easy to determine which generic approach will provide the best results. To obtain optimal results, it may be necessary to try different generic instances. Fortunately, the amount of coding required to change between different instances is fairly minimal.

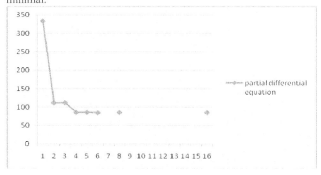

Figure 9 - Partial Differential Equation

(time vs worker count)

This test involves applying the iterative generics to solve a partial differential equation. Unlike the previous tests, the results shown here are for an AMD Athlon II 64 four core processor running on Linux. This is an example measuring the amount of time to complete an embarrassingly parallel application[7] involving 12 levels of nested looping. Parallelism is invoked starting from the outer loops working inwards until all the processors are fully loaded. Beyond that, inner loops are executed sequentially. In this example, the outer loop has 3 iterations, and the next inner loop has 5 iterations. The code chooses worker counts optimal for the number of processors specified. When compiled for two cores, the code

selects a worker count of three, since that is the optimum value for 3 iterations and 2 core. When the two core version of the code runs on a machine with four physical cores however (as shown), the three workers are each allocated a processor, which is why the graph shows the same result when compiled for two processors as for three. When compiled for 4 core, the outermost loop utilizes three workers, since work cannot be divided further between three iterations, while the next inner loop utilizes a worker count of 5 to match the 5 iterations needed. This results in loading all four processors, and generating a better time then the version compiled for 3 processors. Beyond that, compiling the code for a higher number of processors than are actually available does not add any further speed increases, as one would expect.

When the code is run on a dual core processor however (not shown), compiling for two processors generates a suboptimal speed result because two of the three iterations of the outer loop are assigned to one worker. When the first worker completes, the remaining worker still has one iterations worth of work to complete, and for that last iteration, only one of the processors is loaded. Compiling the code for three processors however provides the optimal result, because all three workers are initially given the same amount of work. The three workers migrate as needed between the two physical processors so they progress at the same rate. Consequently, they all complete at the same time, and the processors are fully loaded for the duration of the processing.

Generally it was found that the optimal number of workers for iterative parallelism can be calculated using the following algorithm.

```
if iterations count is significant relative
  to the processor count then
  if iteration count >= processor count then
    select worker count that is the smallest
    factor of the iteration count that is
    >= the number of processors
  else
    use Iteration count
  end if
else use processor count
end if
```

For example, for a quadcore system, the following table can be calculated.

Iteration Count	Recommended Worker Count
3	3
4	4
5	5
6	6
7	7
8	4
9	9
10	5
11	11
12	4

Figure 10 - Optimal Worker counts for quad-core target

As a final example, consider the parallel calculation of Bernoulli numbers. This example is interesting on a number of fronts. For one, an algorithm for calculating Bernoulli numbers is described in note

G in Ada Lovelace's notes from 1842 on Charles Babbage's Analytical engine[9]. The initial idea was to see if the algorithm originally described by Ada Lovelace could be written in Ada, and integrated with the parallelism generics. Upon examining the algorithm involving the method of finite differences however, it became apparent that the algorithm wasn't suitable for parallelism, because results from each iteration relied on results from previous iterations. Today however, numerous algorithms for calculating Bernoulli numbers exist. The Akiyama-Tanagawa algorithm[10] was chosen because it is easy to understand and implement, and because it lends itself towards a parallel approach. Though it may not be the most efficient algorithm, it is suitable for testing the parallelism generics.

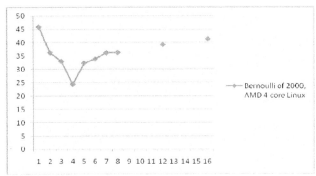

**Figure 11 - Calculate Bernoulli value of 2000
(time vs worker count)**

These tests involved using the GNU Multi Precision library (GMP) [11] big number library, which is a library of functions for performing mathematical functions using arbitrary precision and rational numbers. Addition and multiplication of objects from this library are truly associative as there is no loss in precision, since results are represented as rational numbers. The tests results shown here were also generated on 64 bit Linux using an AMD Athlon II 64 bit processor, which has four cores, and involves measuring the amount of time (in seconds) to calculate the Bernoulli number for 2000. The results show the importance of selecting the correct worker count to match the number of available processors.

10. CONCLUSIONS

The generics presented facilitate adding parallelism to code that otherwise might have been written to execute sequentially. Although these generics are deemed to be useable as is, it is desirable that the parallelism could be specified in a more simpler manner using special parallelism pragmas. Although these pragmas do not exist today, it should be possible to write preprocessor utilities that transpose the pragmas into the generic code without too much difficulty, and without having to modify Ada compiler code.

11. ACKNOWLEDGEMENTS

Thanks to Dr. Jon Squire from the Department of Computer Science and Electrical Engineering of the University of Maryland Baltimore County for providing coding examples for solving matrices and partial differential equations, including matrix solving source code that was written originally in FORTRAN 50 years ago. It was a thrill to apply these generics to real application code, let alone software whose origin goes back to the late 1950's. Indeed it was this spirit of enthusiasm that led to looking back even farther (over 160 years) to the time of Charles Babbage and Ada Lovelace, to see how parallelism today might be applied to the problems that were of interest at that point in time. Thanks must then be given posthumously to Ada Lovelace and Charles Babbage, as without computers, there wouldn't be much to comment on in this paper.

Thanks also to General Dynamics Canada for providing funding for the author to attend the SPAA 2009 conference in Calgary, where the inspiration was found for writing this paper, and developing the software behind the paper.

12. REFERENCES

[1] Frigo M., Halpern P., Leiserson C., and Lewin-Berlin S., Reducers and Other Cilk++ Hyperobjects. *ACM SPAA '09* (2009)

[2] Burns, A., Wellings A., Concurrent and Real-Time Programming in Ada, Cambridge University Press, 2007

[3] Taft, S.T., Duff, R. A., Bruckardt, R.L. And Plödereder, E. Eds (2000). Consolidated Ada Reference Manual. LNCS 2219, Springer-Verlag

[4] Barney Blaise, Lawrence Livermore National Laboratory, https://computing.llnl.gov/tutorials/openMP/#WorkSharing (Sept 2010)

[5] Kaiser, C., Fradat-Peyre, J-F., Évangelista, S., Rousseau P., C# and Ada Monitors queuing policies : a case study and its Ada refinement. ACM Sigada Ada Letters, 24, 2, pp. 23-37 August 2006.

[6] Association for Computing Machinery (ACM) SigAda, ASIS Working Group, http://www.sigada.org/wg/asiswg/, Sept 2010

[7] Fox, G., Williams, R., Messina G., Parallel Computing Works!, **ISBN 1-55860-253-4** Morgan Kaufmann Publishers, **Inc. 1994**

[8] Walker J., Red Black Trees, http://www.eternallyconfuzzled.com/tuts/datastructures/jsw_tut_rbtree.aspx (Aug 2010)

[9] Menabrea, L.F., Lovelace A., Sketch of the Analytical Engine Invented by Charles Babbage, *Bibliothèque Universelle de Genève*, October, 1842, No. 82

[10] Kaneko M., The Akiyama-Tanigawa algorithm for Bernoulli Numbers, Journal of Integer Sequences, Vol 3 (2000), Article 00.2.9

[11] Free Software Foundation, GMP, http://gmplib.org, Sept 2010

Extending Ada to Support Multi-core Based Monitoring and Fault Tolerance*

You Li[1,2]
leo86@seg.nju.edu.cn

Lu Yang[3,1]
yanglu@suda.edu.cn

Lei Bu[1,2]
bl@seg.nju.edu.cn

Linzhang Wang[1,2]
lzwang@nju.edu.cn

Jianhua Zhao[1,2]
zhaojh@nju.edu.cn

Xuandong Li[1,2]
lxd@nju.edu.cn

[1]State Key Laboratory of Novel Software Technology, Nanjing University, Nanjing, Jiangsu, P.R.China 210093
[2]Department of Computer Science and Technology, Nanjing University, Nanjing, Jiangsu, P.R.China 210093
[3]School of Computer Science and Technology, Soochow University, Suzhou, Jiangsu, P.R.China 215006

ABSTRACT

Monitoring-Oriented Programming (MOP) and Software Fault Tolerance(SFT) are two important approaches to guarantee the reliablity of software systems, especially for those running online for long term. However, the introduction of monitoring or fault tolerance module will bring in high overhead. With the prevalence of multi-core platform, we can find the trade off between the reliablity and the efficiency. As one of the most reliable programming languages, Ada is used to a significant degree in many fields. Providing the support of MOP and SFT in Ada can help the programmers enhance the reliablity of software systems. In this paper, we present an approach to extending Ada to support multi-core based monitoring and fault tolerance. First we introduce the framework of multi-core based MOP and SFT. Based on this framework, programmers can design the components of MOP and SFT with tasks parallel to main tasks in Ada programming. All these tasks can be allocated to different physical cores to run concurrently. Then, we give a proposal for enabling multi-core based MOP and SFT in Ada. In this proposal, we design two packages *System.MOP_Elements* and *System.SFT_Elements* for programmers to indicate various monitoring and fault tolerance components. With the packages, programmers can also assign computation resources for each component. Finally we animate this proposal via a prototype tool called MCAda and use two case studies to show our approach.

Categories and Subject Descriptors

D.2.4 [**Software Engineering**]: Software/Program Verification—*Reliablity,Validation*; D.2.3 [**Software Engineering**]: Coding Tools and Techniques

*This work is supported by the National Natural Science Foundation of China (No.90818022, No.60721002), the National Grand Fundamental Research 973 Program of China (No.2009CB320702), and by the National S&T Major Project (2009z01036-001-001-3).

General Terms

Design, Reliablity

Keywords

multi-core,monitoring-oriented programming, software fault tolerance

1. INTRODUCTION

With the development of software industry, the reliablity of software attracts more and more attentions. Various approaches are being proposed to enhance the reliablity of software systems. Monitoring Oriented Programming (MOP) and Software Fault Tolerance (SFT), which can give high confidence for long-running online software system to run correctly, are becoming prior choices for developers to design and develop reliable software systems.

The main purpose of Ada is to develop software system with long-life and high reliability. Here we list some of the fields in which Ada is used to a significant degree[4]:

1) Air Traffic Management System
2) Commercial Aviation
3) Railway Transportation
4) Commercial Rockets
5) Commercial Imaging Space Vehicles
6) Communication and Navigational Satellites and Receivers
7) Scientific Space Vehicles
8) Banking and Financial Systems
9) Information Systems
10) Military Applications

In all these fields, the software systems are safety-critical and running online for long term, a tiny error may cause great losses. Therefore, we need more ways to increase the reliability of these systems. MOP and SFT can play important roles to guarantee the system to run correctly. Consequently, we can introduce MOP and SFT mechanisms into Ada for better performance on software reliablity.

However, these approaches may introduce high overhead, which causes the loss of efficiency. For MOP, programmers introduce components for monitoring, analysis, error handling and so on, these components may result in over consumption of computing resources. For SFT, no matter multi-version techniques[7, 1, 8] or single-version techniques[5], the redundant versions for key units or check points for self-checking will multiply the execution time of the system, which may bring on great losses in some real time systems.

To maintain the efficiency, we need some ways to reduce such overhead or make the overhead acceptable. The prevalence of multi-core platform provides us a chance to implement efficient MOP and SFT systems. For MOP, we can allocate the target tasks and the monitoring tasks to separate physical cores, make them run concurrently. For SFT, different versions of a key unit can be executed concurrently in different physical cores, which can improve the efficiency of an SFT system. Therefore, the multi-core platform is a good stage for MOP and SFT system developing.

However, most software developers may not be familiar with the programming details of multi-core platforms. They should focus on how to design monitoring and fault tolerance modules, but not how to assign these tasks to multi-core platforms. Methods to allocate the monitoring components and the fault tolerance modules to multi-core architectures automatically can help the programmers deal with the problem.

For the reasons above, we design some new packages in Ada, which provide support for multi-core based MOP and SFT. The programmers can use these packages to declare different tasks of the monitoring and fault tolerance modules, meanwhile, they can indicate the computation resource requirement of each task, the packages will allocate the tasks to different physical cores automatically with the guidance of the requirements.

The contributions of the paper are as follows:

- We propose two packages *System.MOP_Elements* and *System.SFT_Elements*, which extend Ada to support multi-core based MOP and SFT programming. The packages provide interfaces for programmers to develop MOP and SFT systems in multi-core platform.

- Our proposal can support applications migrating to different multi-core platforms with different number of physical cores. The programmers only need to indicate the computation resource requirement of each task in monitoring or fault tolerance modules, and the physical cores allocation of each task will be generated automatically.

- A tool called MCAda is implemented to support animating the two packages. Also we conduct two case studies to demonstrate that multi-core based MOP and SFT can make the program more reliable without losing too much efficiency.

The structure of this paper is as follows. In Section 2, we introduce the framework of multi-core based MOP and SFT. In Section 3, we represent the packages we proposed for enabling multi-core based MOP and SFT in Ada. In Section 4, we illustrate how to animate the packages. Then we use two case studies to show how we can develop multi-core based MOP and SFT program in Ada. In Section 5, we discuss the task affinity problem in multi-core dependent programming. In the last section, we present the conclusions.

2. BACKGROUND

In our previous work[11, 10, 12], we proposed the framework of multi-core based MOP and SFT. In this section, we will give a brief introduction about multi-core based MOP and SFT.

2.1 Multi-core Based MOP

Monitoring-Oriented Programming, which is viewed as a lightweighted formal method, is mostly used for runtime verification. Here we quote the definition of MOP[3]:

- "Monitoring-Oriented Programming (MOP) is a formal framework for software development and analysis, in which the developer specifies desired properties using definable specification formalisms, along with code to execute when properties are violated or validated."

Traditional off-line verification techniques may have some limitation, such as state explosion problem, in industry. MOP is a complement for these off-line verification techniques, for it can be used for the online verification. However, the problem of MOP is loss of coverage. MOP can be used to give high confidence to the system, but we can not use it to prove the correctness of a system. Most of the time, we can use MOP for a target system which will online for long term and can not be shut down, for example, the navigation system for an aeroplane. With a monitor we can find the trend of failure and prevent errors.

Generally, the design of MOP includes the following steps:

1. Instrumenting: The target system is instrumented in this step. The instrumented units will indicate the variables and properties to be monitored, then they will collect the runtime information of these variables and properties when the instrumented version of the target system is executing.

2. Monitoring: In this step, monitors are constructed. A monitor is composed of three units: monitoring unit, analysis unit and handler unit. The monitoring unit capture the information collected by the instrumented unit, the analysis unit then analyze the information to determine whether the variables and properties are validated or violated.

3. Handling: This step is to handle the result of the analysis unit. The handler unit can execute feedback actions, give a warning and record the information.

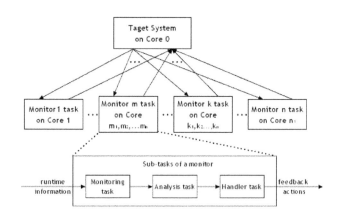

Figure 1: Multi-core Based MOP

In multi-core architecture, the target system and all monitors can be mapped into different physical cores. There are two methods to optimize MOP in multi-core platform:

- Design the monitor separately according to their functions and purposes. Different properties or variables can be analyzed by different monitors.

- The monitor can be decomposed into several subtasks, including the monitoring task, the analysis task and the handler task.These subtasks can be executed on different cores and cooperate through a pipeline.

The framework of multi-core based MOP is shown in Figure 1. There are n monitoring tasks to check different properties of the target system, which is allocated to run on core 0. In addition, the monitor task m, which has several subtasks, is allocated to core $m_1, m_2, \ldots, m_n$, subtasks of a monitor can be allocated to different cores.

2.2 Multi-core Based SFT

Software fault tolerance(SFT) techniques learn the experience from the hardware fault tolerance. It provides the system the ability to detect the errors and recover from failure, which can ensure the system to run as specified. The basic idea of software fault tolerance is to create redundant versions of the key units of the system, which can be used to compensate or mask software failures.

Current main approaches of software fault tolerance including multi-version techniques and single-version techniques. The multi-version techniques include Recovery block[7], N-version programming[1] and Consensus recovery blocks[8]; Single-version techniques include Self-checking[5] programming and so on.

Among the approaches of SFT, the N-version programming technique is quite suitable to be implemented in multi-core architecture. In an N-version software system, key units of the software are implemented in n separate versions ($n \geq 2$). Considering the cost and efficiency, only some key units of the system are developed in multiple versions. For each key unit, the n versions are implemented in diverse ways and accomplish equivalent task. In order to tolerate design faults, each version of the key unit is developed by independent groups. With the design diversity technique[2], all versions are functional equivalent but structural diverse, in order to avoid the similar fault modules. When the system is executing an key unit, each version will submit its result to a decision component to determine a correct result of the key unit.

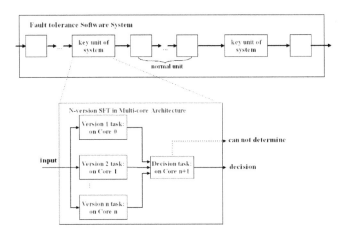

Figure 2: Multi-core Based SFT

In multi-core based SFT, each version of the key unit and the decision unit can be designed as a single task. All this tasks can be assigned to different cores to run concurrently when the key unit is executing(Figure 2).

3. ENABLING MULTI-CORE BASED MOP AND SFT IN ADA

To support multi-core based MOP and SFT in Ada, we should implement each component for monitoring and fault tolerance as independent task unit first. In this paper we design two new packages, *System.MOP_Elements* and *System.SFT_Elements*, which help the programmers allocate the tasks for the monitoring and fault tolerance to multi-core architecture. The new packages have the features below:

- Helping developers identify or indicate different components of MOP and SFT. For example, in MOP, developers can indicate the target unit and the corresponding monitor; In SFT, different versions of different key units can be identified by the procedures provided by the packages.

- Providing a high level abstract methods for developers to indicate their plan for allocating the tasks for monitoring and fault to physical cores. The developers do not have to know the exact architecture of the underlying hardware, which can make them focus on the design of MOP and SFT system.

3.1 Multi-core programming in Ada

In Ada, the task unit is a natural support for parallel programming, which can be used in implementation of the multi-core based MOP and SFT systems. The components of monitoring and fault tolerance module can be designed as separate tasks.

Here we quotes the explanation in the Ada Reference Manual, which illustrate the relationship between Ada program and multi-core platform.

- "NOTES1 Concurrent task execution may be implemented on multicomputers, multiprocessors, or with interleaved execution on a single physical processor. On the other hand, whenever an implementation can determine that the required semantic effects can be achieved when parts of the execution of a given task are performed by different physical processors acting in parallel, it may choose to perform them in this way."-Section 9 par 11

- "In a multiprocessor system, a task can be on the ready queues of more than one processor. At the extreme, if several sharing one ready queue, and can be implemented that way. Thus, the dispatching model covers multi-processors where dispatching is implemented using a single ready queue, as well as those with separate dispatching domains."-D.2.1 par 15

These two explanations illustrate that the Ada can provide the fundamental support for parallel programming in multi-core platform by using task units. However, Ada can not support the developers to allocate tasks to processors, which may help the developers to implement multi-core based MOP and SFT system better.

In 2007, A.J.Wellings and A.Burns argue that Ada should provide more explicit support for multiprocessor system[9]. They proposed a new package *System.Processor_Element*, which captures the interface between developers and the underlying system's multiprocessor architectures, to integrate multiprocessor support into Ada. With this package, the affinity of the tasks can be set by programmers.

In this paper, we use the package *System.Processor_Element* as a fundamental support for multi-core based MOP and SFT to allocate the tasks for monitoring or fault tolerance to processors in different multi-core architectures.

```
with System.Processor_Element; use System.Processor_Element;
with Ada.Task_Identification; use Ada.Task_Identification;
package System.MOP_Elements is

   Monitor_Affinity_Error : exception;
   -- Monitor_Affinity_Error will be raised when there are conflicts in task affinity

   procedure Set_Monitor_Task(TID: in Task_Id := Current_Task; Processors: in Processor_Set:= Available_Processors;
                              Monitor_ID: in Natural; Virtual_Core: in Natural)
   -- set a particular task to be a monitor task, indicate the computation source needed

   procedure Set_Analysis_Task(TID: in Task_Id := Current_Task; Processors: in Processor_Set:= Available_Processors;
                               Monitor_ID: in Natural; Virtual_Core: in Natural)
   -- set a particular task to be a analysis task, indicate the computation source needed

   procedure Set_Handler_Task(TID: in Task_Id := Current_Task; Processors: in Processor_Set:= Available_Processors;
                              Monitor_ID: in Natural; Virtual_Core: in Natural)
   -- set a particular task to be a handler task, indicate the computation source needed

   procedure Set_Target_Task(TID: in Task_Id := Current_Task; Processors: in Processor_Set:= Available_Processors;
                             Virtual_Core: in Natural)
   -- set a particular task to be the target task, indicate the computation source needed
```

Figure 3: The package*System.MOP_Elements*

3.2 The Virtual Core

When some developers develop a MOP or SFT system, they may be unfamiliar with the programming details of the underlying multi-core architecture, for example, the number of the physical cores or how to allocate the tasks to processors. Here we provide a method for developers to express their requirements for computation resource. Developers can use a variable called *Virtual_Core* in the packages we propose to present the computation resource each task of the MOP or SFT system requests. Programmers provide the virtual cores needed by the tasks of monitoring and fault tolerance modules , then the physical cores assignment will be computed with the guidance of the virtual cores requirements, and tasks will be allocated to the physical cores automatically. Thus the developers' requirement will be satisfied no matter the number of physical cores is more or less than the number of virtual cores, which can make them pay more attention on the MOP and SFT design.

3.3 System.MOP_Elements

To support MOP in multi-core architecture, we design the package *System.MOP_Element* (Figure 3). The package provides four procedures for the developers. As we mentioned in Section 2.1, in a system using MOP, there are a target system, and k monitors(or sub-monitors) with a monitoring task, an analysis task and a handler task. The four procedures in the package are provided for programmers to develop multi-core based MOP systems.

The procedure *Set_Monitor_Task* is used to indicate which task is set to be the monitoring unit. The developers can use this procedure to indicate a monitoring unit of a monitor. Meanwhile, the procedure can also be used to indicate a lightweight monitor task with the analysis unit and handler unit in it.

There are four parameters in the procedure *Set_Monitor_Task*. The parameter *TID* indicates which task is set to be the monitor(or monitoring unit) of a multi-core based MOP system. The default value of *TID* is the *Task_Id* of current task. Programmers can call the procedure in the beginning of a task body statement with the default *TID*, which can set the current task to be the monitor component.

The type of the parameter *Processors* is *Processor_Set*, which is declared in the package *System.Processor_Element*[9]. It is an array of Boolean. An element set to *True*, indicates that the corresponding processor is included in the set. This parameter indicates the processors assigned to the monitor component of the MOP system. The default value of *Processors* is *Available_Processors*, which is got from the package *System.Processor_Element* and indicates that which of the processors in the system are current available to the program. Besides, the programmers can schedule the task affinity manually by providing a *Processor_Set*. However, the task affinity set manually must be a subset of the available processors set. Otherwise *Monitor_Affinity_Error* will be raised.

The parameter *Monitor_Id* indicates which monitor the task of MOP belongs to. It can help the programmers identify which property or variable being monitored is violated. The tasks with the same *Monitor_Id* should be assigned the same *Processor_Set*, else the package can not automatically allocating the tasks to physical cores and *Monitor_Affinity_Error* will be raised.

The parameter *Virtual_Core* indicates how many virtual cores are needed for the task, as Section 3.2 mentions. With the guide of *Virtual_Core*, the task affinity will be calculated and the task can be allocated to physical cores automatically.

In Section 2.1, we propose two methods to optimize MOP in multi-core platform. The second method is to decompose the monitoring task into several subtasks(including the monitoring task, analysis task and the handler task) and allocating the subtasks to different cores, which can make the subtasks cooperate through

```
with System.Processor_Element; use System.Processor_Element;
with Ada.Task_Identification; use Ada.Task_Identification;
package System.SFT_Elements is

    Fault_Tolerance_Affinity_Error : exception;
    - - Fault_Tolerance_Affinity_Error will be raised when there are conflicts in task affinity

    procedure Set_Fault_Tolerance_Task(TID: in Task_Id := Current_Task;
                                        Processors: in Processor_Set := Available_Processors;
                                        Virtual_Core: in Natural;
                                        Unit_Number: in Natural;
                                        Version_Number: in Natural)
    - - set a particular task to be one version of a key unit, indicate the computation source needed

    procedure Set_Decision_Task(TID: in Task_Id := Current_Task;
                                 Processors: in Processor_Set := Available_Processors;
                                 Virtual_Core: in Natural;
                                 Unit_Number: in Natural)
    - - set a particular task to be the decision unit of a key unit,indicate the computation source needed
```

Figure 4: The package *System.SFT_Elements*

a pipeline. Therefore, the package provide other two procedures *Set_Analysis_Task* and *Set_Handler_Task*, which set a task to be the analysis subtask or handler subtask. Same as the procedure *Set_Monitor_Task*, the two procedures can help the developers indicate which monitor the subtask of MOP belongs to and how many virtual cores are provided for the subtask.

The procedure *Set_Target_Task* is used to set a task to be the target system. Because we assume that there is only one target system in an MOP system, the target system doesn't need the parameter *Monitor_Id*. The developer can use this procedure to provide the virtual cores assignment for the target system.

3.4 System.SFT_Elements

To support multi-core based SFT, we design the package *System.SFT_Elements*(Figure 4). In a fault tolerance software system, there are k key units. Each key unit is implemented in n versions. To support N-version SFT module, we also need some methods to indicate the decision unit. There are two procedures in the package*System.SFT_Elements*, which can help the programmers to indicate the function and the computation resource requirement of a task of the multi-core based SFT module.

The procedure *Set_Fault_Tolerance_Task* have 5 parameters. The parameter *TID* indicates which task is the redundant version of the SFT system. The parameter *Processors* indicates the processor(s) assigned to the fault tolerance component of the SFT system. The parameter *Virtual_Core* indicates the virtual cores assignment for the fault tolerance task. The three parameters play the same role as the parameters of the same name in the package *System.MOP_Elements*.

The parameter *Unit_Number* indicates the key unit of the fault tolerance task. We assume that different key units are executing on different stages of the software system and the tasks in a key unit do not interfere the physical cores assignment of other key units. This parameter is used to identify the same key unit of the redundant version of the fault tolerance task, so we calculate the allocation of the tasks in SFT module for each key unit sepa-

rately. Similar to the parameter *Monitor_ID* in the package *System.MOP_Elements*, the tasks with the same *Unit_Number* should be assigned the same *Processors*, otherwise the procedure can not calculate how to mapping the virtual cores to the physical cores and *Fault_Tolerance_Affinity_Error* will be raised.

The parameter *Version_Number* is used to distinguish the fault tolerance tasks of the key unit. The developers should assign an unique *Version_Number* value to each fault tolerance task of the same key unit. And this parameter can be used for the decision unit to identify the error version.

The other procedure *Set_Decision_Task* is used to set a task to be the decision unit of a key unit of an SFT system. Similar to the procedure *Set_Fault_Tolerance_Task*, developer can decide the virtual cores assignment and physical core affinity of a decision task.

3.5 How to use System.MOP_Elements and System.SFT_Elements

With the help of the packages *System.MOP_Elements* and *System.SFT_Elements*, the programmers can convert a program into multi-core based MOP or SFT program.

There are 2 steps to convert exist programs to a multi-core based MOP or SFT program:

- Develop the components of the monitoring and fault tolerance module using the task unit. For monitoring, programmers can develop a light weight monitor with monitoring, analysis and handler in one task, or implement each component using a single task, also they should instrument the target system to declare the variables and properties to be monitored. For fault tolerance, programmers can develop redundant versions of the key unit and a decision unit, each of unit should be implement as a task.

- Use the procedures in the package *System.MOP_Elements* and *System.SFT_Elements* to indicate the function and the virtual cores assignment of each task.

After converting the program, the procedures in *System.MOP_Ele -ments* and *System.SFT_Elements* will calculate the mapping strategy from virtual cores to physical cores. Then the procedures call the *System.Processor_Element* [9] to allocate the tasks to the processors in different multi-core architectures. The principle to use the package *System.MOP_Elements* and *System.SFT_Elements* is shown in Figure 5

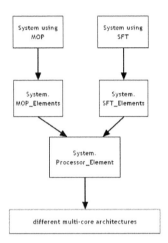

Figure 5: The principle to use System.MOP_Elements and System.SFT_Elements

4. ANIMATION OF PROPOSAL

In this section, we illustrate how we animate multi-core based MOP and SFT approaches in Ada. We use the Windows API to simulate the package *System.Processor_Element*, then we develop a tool MCAda to convert the source code files using the packages *System.MOP_Elements* and *System.SFT_Elements*. Compilable source codes will be generated by the tool, which animates multi-core based MOP and SFT in Ada.

4.1 Allocating Task to Processor

Because Ada provides no direct support for controlling which tasks are mapped to which physical cores, we need some other methods to help the developers to allocate the tasks to the physical cores. Here we use Windows Thread API[6] to simulate the functions in the package *System.Processor_Element* [9].

The Windows Thread API provide some functions for developers to control the affinity mask for threads and processes, the functions contains,

- *SetProcessAffinityMask*: this function sets a processor affinity mask for the threads of the specified process. A process affinity mask is a bit vector in which each bit represents the processors that a process is allowed to run on.

- *GetProcessAffinityMask*: this function retrieves the process affinity mask for the specified process and the system affinity mask for the system. A system affinity mask is a bit vector in which each bit represents the processors that are configured into a system.

- *SetThreadAffinityMask*: this function sets a processor affinity ask for the specified thread. A thread affinity mask is a bit

vector in which each bit represents a logical processor that a thread is allowed to run on.

The value of the process affinity mask must be a subset of the system affinity mask, which means a process is only allowed to run on the processors configured into a system. Similarly, a thread affinity mask must be a subset of the process affinity mask for the containing process of a thread. A thread can only run on the processors its process can run on.

For example, if the value of affinity mask is 1(2#0001#), it is related to Core 0 of the CPU, the value 2(2#0010#) is related to Core 1, the value 3(2#0011#)is related to Core 0 and Core 1, the value 4(2#0100#)is related to Core 2, and the rest may be deduced by analogy.

```
_declspec (dllexport)  int   Set_Thread_Affinity_Mask
                              (DWORD dwThreadAffinityMask)
{

    DWORD  s_TID = GetCurrentThreadId();
    HANDLE  hThread  = OpenThread
                    (PROCESS_ALL_ACCESS,TRUE,s_TID);
    SetThreadAffinityMask(hThread,dwThreadAffinityMask);

    return 0;

};
```

Figure 6: The Program Set_Thread_Affinity_Mask in C++

```
package Task_Affinity is

    procedure Set_Affinity_Mask(Affinity:Long_Integer);

    pragma linker_option("TaskAffinity.dll");

    pragma import(C_Plus_Plus, Set_Task_Affinity_Mask,
                "Set_Thread_Affinity_Mask");

end Task_Affinity;
```

Figure 7: The package *Task_Affinity*

For Ada, a task is related to a thread in Windows, and an executable unit is mapped to a process. Ada provides some facilities for interfacing with the C and C++ language in Annex B, we can use the pragma *Import, Linker_options* to call the functions developed by C or C++. In this paper, we develop a simple function to support the task allocation using the API *SetThreadAffinityMask*.

Firstly, we develop a C++ program, which has a function called *Set_Thread_Affinity_Mask*(Figure 6). The program is compiled as a Dynamic Link Library(DLL) file. Then we develop a package *Task_Affinity*(Figure 7) to import the function in the DLL. The programmers can call the procedure *Set_Task_Affinity_Mask* in the package *Task_Affinity* to allocated to the processor according to the variable *Affinity*.

4.2 Tool support for Animation

In order to support animating multi-core based MOP and SFT approaches in Ada, we develop a tool called MCAda. The work flow of MCAda is shown in Figure 8. The developers can call the procedures in the packages *System.MOP_Elements* and *System.SFT_Elements* to indicate which task is the component of the monitoring or fault tolerance and how many virtual cores are needed in their source code. Then they can input the source code to MCAda and provide the number of physical cores of the multi-core architecture. MCAda can handle the source code and generate the new code using the package in Section 4.1 to allocate the tasks for MOP and SFT to physical cores.

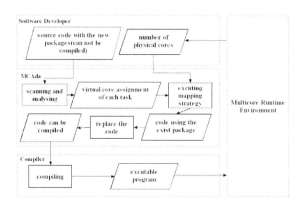

Figure 8: The Work Flow Of MCAda

MCAda deals with the input in three steps:

First, it scans the source code to locate the places using the functions in the packages we proposed in Section 3 and get the information of the virtual core assignment of all the MOP and SFT tasks.

Second, it generates the physical core assignment scheme with the instruction of the virtual cores assignment and the number of physical cores. Here we give the pseudo code of the algorithm for the strategy of the assignment scheme in Figure 9.

The input of this algorithm are the list of the virtual cores assigned to each task for MOP or SFT, and the number of physical cores. The output is a list of physical core assignment indices for all these tasks. The algorithm first sums the total number of the virtual cores assigned. Then it calculates the number of physical cores of each task, according to the virtual core proportion of the task. After that, it sorts the tasks according to the number of physical core assigned in ascending order. Finally, it uses greedy algorithm to calculate the physical core assignment indices for each task.With the physical core assignment indices, we can calculate affinity mask of each task.

Third, it replaces the statements which call the procedures about multi-core based MOP and SFT with the procedure in the package *Task_Affinity*, using the affinity mask calculated in Step 2. The output of MCAda is the code with the physical cores assignment scheme, it can be compiled and executed on multi-core platform. Figure 10 shows how the MCAda help the programmers to animate the packages *System.MOP_Elements* and *System.SFT_Elements*.

4.3 Case Study

To show how to implement MOP and SFT in multi-core architectures, we designed two experiments. The case *Elevator System* is an implementation of MOP in multi-core platforms. The case *Interpolation Unit* shows how to implement SFT system in multi-core platforms.

The processor for the experiments is Intel Core 2 Quad Q6600

```
- -calculate the total of the virtual cores
for (each tasks for MOP or SFT) loop
      SumVirturalCoreNum := SumVirturalCoreNum +
                              task(i).virtual_core;
end loop;

- -calculate the physical core number of each task
for(each task for MOP or SFT) loop
      task(i).physical_core = Physical_Core_Num *
                  task(i).virtual_core / SumVirturalCoreNum
end loop;

- -sort the tasks according to the physical cores
- -in ascending order
Sort(tasks.physical_core);

- -calculate the physical core indexed for each task
Used:Float := 0;
From_Index,To_Index: Integer := 0;
for (each tasks for MOP or SFT) loop
      Used:=Used + task(i).physical_core;
      To_Index := Upbound(Used);
      task(i).set_physical_core_index(From_Index,To_index);
      if (Used = To_Index) then
            From_Index:=To_Index;
      end if;
end loop;
```

Figure 9: Algorithm for Mapping Strategy

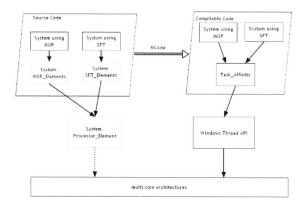

Figure 10: Using MCAda to Convert the Source code

(2.4GHz/4MB*2L2/1066MHz). The operating system is Windows Vista.

4.3.1 The Elevator System

In order to show the implementation of multi-core based MOP, we designed a simulate elevator system. The elevator system is composed of three parts: a package *ELEVATOR*, which provides the command to control the elevator; a task *REQUEST_DB*, which receives the requests of passengers, controls the elevator and calculates the destination; a task *ELEVATOR_CONTROL*, which responses passengers' requests and controls the elevator.

The tasks *REQUEST_DB* and *ELEVATOR_CONTROL* communicate with each other in order to :1) analyze the requests of the

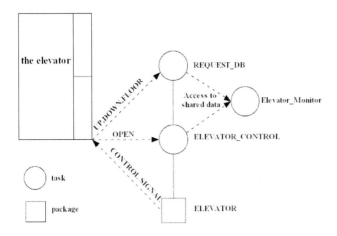

Figure 11: The Structure of the Elevator System with Monitor

tor_Monitor, the new statement is *Set_Thread_Affinity_Mask(8)*,which allocates the main task to physical core 4 (Figure 12).

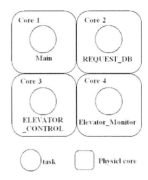

Figure 12: The allocation of the tasks

Figure 13 shows some records wrote by the monitor system. We can see the data race is observed and recorded.

```
D:\Research\ada\WorkSpace\test2\Build\run_elevator
There is Data Race in DOWN_REQUEST between floor 2 and floor 1
There is Data Race in DOWN_REQUEST between floor 2 and floor 1
There is Data Race in DOWN_REQUEST between floor 5 and floor 2
There is Data Race in DOWN_REQUEST between floor 5 and floor 1
There is Data Race in UP_REQUEST between floor 7 and floor 1
There is Data Race in UP_REQUEST between floor 7 and floor 1
There is Data Race in DOWN_REQUEST between floor 6 and floor 5
There is Data Race in DOWN_REQUEST between floor 6 and floor 1
There is Data Race in DOWN_REQUEST between floor 2 and floor 6
There is Data Race in UP_REQUEST between floor 4 and floor 7
```

Figure 13: The Record of the Monitor

passengers and determine the next destination of the elevator. 2) provide the information of the floor been served.

To show how we can use the package *System.MOP_Element* to develop a multi-core based MOP system, we injected some errors to the elevator system. We didn't use the protected object to deal with the shared data between the task *REQUEST_DB* and *ELE-VATOR_CONTROL*, so when the requests from passengers reach a certain amount, the data race problem may cause a unstable constitution of the elevator.

In order to find the data race problem, we added a monitor task called *Elevator_Monitor* to the target system, which monitors the access to the shared data. When the monitor finds there are more than one tasks are going to access the shared data and at least one access is writing, it will raise a warning when the data race problem happens. The elevator system with monitor is shown in Figure 11.

As mentioned in Section 2.1, we instrumented the target system, and the instrument unit will record the access type and object of the shared data when the target system is running. Then the monitor will scan the record to analyze whether there is data race. Once a data race happens, the monitor will record the object which cause the data race.

Because the monitor may write and read the record frequently, we allocate the monitor task to a single physical core to avoid affecting the executing of the target system.

We can call the procedures in the package *System.MOP_Element* to assign the virtual cores to the tasks. For the task *REQUEST_DB* and *ELEVATOR_CONTROL* and the main task, we add the statement calling the procedure *Set_Target_Task(Virtual_Core=>1)* to the beginning of the statement of each task body. For the task *Elevator_Monitor*, we add the statement calling the procedure *Set_Monitor_Task(Monitor_ID=>1,Virtual_Core=>1)* to the beginning of the statement of task body.

Then we used the tool MCAda to scan the source files with statement calling the procedure in the package *System.MOP_Element* and generated the new code using the package in Section 4.1.

For the main task, the new statement is *Set_Thread_Affinity_Mask(1)*, which allocates the main task to physical core 1; for the task *RE-QUEST_DB*, the new statement is *Set_Thread_Affinity_Mask(2)*, which allocates the main task to physical core 2; for the task *ELE-VATOR_CONTROL*, the new statement is *Set_Thread_Affinity_Mask(4)*, which allocates the main task to physical core 3; for the task *Eleva-*

4.3.2 The Interpolation Unit

Interpolation method is in the mathematical subfield of numerical analysis. It can constructs new data points within the range of a discrete set of known data points.

The interpolation method is widely used in engineering and science. In science, people often have a group of data points, which are obtained by sampling or experimentation, they try to construct a function which closely fits the data points to predict other data points. In engineering, we often need a computer program to control the machining of a machine element. There may be only some data points to indicate shape of the machine element on design stage. On machining stage, the program use the interpolation methods to calculate other data points of the shape to control the cutter to machining a smooth machine elements. In that case, the unit to implement the interpolation methods is a key point of the control program.

In this experiment, we designed an interpolation unit with SFT method. The interpolation unit uses polynomial interpolation method to calculate the points of a curve in a rectangular cartesian coordinate system. Assume we have k points in the coordinate which are $P_1(x_1, y_1), P_2(x_2, y_2), \ldots, P_k(x_k, y_k)$, where $x_1 < x_2 < x_k$, we can generate a polynomial interpolation with the k point and then calculate the value of a point with a given x.

There are many algorithms to implement polynomial interpolation. We chose three algorithms to develop different versions of the interpolation unit:

a.Lagrange polynomial interpolation:

$$L_n(x) = \sum_{k=0}^{n} \frac{\omega_{n+1}(x)}{(x - x_k)\omega'_{n+1}(x_k)}$$

where $\omega_{n+1}(x) = (x - x_0)(x - x_1)\ldots(x - x_n)$ and
$\omega'_{n+1}(x_k) = (x_k - x_0)\ldots(x_k - x_{k-1})(x_k - x_{k+1})\ldots(x_k - x_n)$

b. Neville successive linear interpolation:

$$I_{0,1,\ldots,k+1}(x) = I_{0,1,\ldots,k}(x) + \frac{I_{1,\ldots,k+1}(x) - I_{0,1,\ldots,k}(x)}{x_{k+1} - x_0}(x - x_0)$$

where $I_{i_1\ldots i_n}(x)$ is the $n - 1$ times polynomial interpolation of function $f(x)$ with the points $P_{i_1}(x_{i_1}, y_{i_1}), P_{i_2}(x_{i_2}, y_{i_2}), \ldots, P_{i_k}(x_{i_k}, y_{i_k})$

c. Newton interpolation formula:

$$N_n(x) = f(x_0) + f[x_0, x_1](x - x_0) + f[x_0, x_1, x_2](x - x_0)(x - x_1) + \ldots + f[x_0, \ldots, x_n](x - x_0)\ldots(x - x_{n-1})$$

where $f[x_0, x_1, \ldots, x_k] = \sum_{j=0}^{k} \frac{f(x_j)}{(x_j - x_0)\ldots(x_j - x_{j-1})(x_j - x_{j+1})\ldots(x_j - x_k)}$

The three algorithms were implemented in three tasks, we also developed a decision function to determine the output of the interpolation units. We assume that the results of two algorithms are consistent when the error of them is less than a given delta which is trivial. If the results of two or more algorithms are consistent, the decision function will return the mean value of the consistent results, else the decision function can not determine a correct output for the interpolation unit, and it will invoke the exception handler.

We used two groups of experiments to show the effect of SFT in multi-core. In group 1, we design 3 experiments: in experiment 1, we executed only one task on one physical core; In experiment 2, we executed three versions of the unit, and each task is allocated to different physical cores to run concurrently; In experiment 3, we allocated three tasks to one physical core. Each experiment calculated 5 hundred million points in a given region. We recorded the computing time for each experiment.

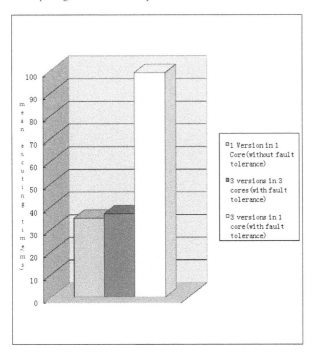

Figure 14: The Mean Time to Run the Interpolation Unit

Figure 14 shows the result of the experiments in group 1. The mean executing time for experiment 1 is 34.7794s. In experiment

2, the result is 36.7161s. In experiment 3, the result is 99.9141s. We can see the cost for fault tolerance is (36.7161 ms - 34.7794ms) ÷ 34.7794 ms = 5.57% , and the speed up from single-core to multi-core is 99.9141 ms ÷ 36.7161 ms = 2.72.

In group 2, we designed two experiments: the experiments inject errors into one/two version, which can check the ability of the SFT system to detect and recover from failures.

Table 1: Result of The Interpolation Unit(1 Incorrect Version)

Algorithm	Result	Validity
Lagrange	3.30694E-1	Error
Neville	3.30374E-1	Correct
Newton	3.30374E-1	Correct
Output	3.30374E-1	Correct

Table 2: Result of The Interpolation Unit(2 Incorrect Versions)

Algorithm	Result	Validity
Lagrange	3.30694E-1	Error
Neville	3.30374E-1	Error
Newton	3.30514E-1	Error
Output	Can't Determine	Error

Table 1 and Table 2 show the results of group 2 of experiments. In Table 1, the error in the Lagrange Polynomial Interpolation is detected and the output is correct. In Table 2, because there are no consistent results, the decision unit can not determine the output and it invokes the exception handler.

5. DISCUSSION

Affinity indicates the relationship between tasks and CPU cores. Most of the time, the allocation of the tasks to physical cores is scheduled by the operating system, which called soft affinity. General speaking, soft affinity have good performance on scheduling the allocation of the tasks to cores. However, sometimes the developers need to manually set the affinity when they can assure that doing so can provide a better performance. The affinity set manually is called hard affinity. Choosing the affinity style is a problem to be considered when develop program on multi-core platform.

In this paper, we propose two packages to introduce a basic support for multi-core based MOP and SFT in Ada. Our proposal can help programmers develop software systems with hard affinity. However, not every scenario is suitable for hard affinity, the developers can choose hard affinity when they can assure the affinity they set can improve the performance of the program, comparing to the automatic scheduling by the operating system.

Based on our knowledge and experience, we summarize some scenarios in which the performance of hard affinity is better:

- One scenario is to develop the system which is long-running and time-sensitive. The developers can use hard affinity to allocate such application to one or a group of cores to monopolize all the computation resource, while allowing the normal scheduling needs on the other cores. Multi-core based MOP is one example of this scenario, for the target system is always long-running and time-sensitive. Developers can use the package *System.MOP_Elements* to set the affinity of the target system and the monitor units to obtain a better performance.

- Another scenario to use hard affinity is the application causing a large amount of computing tasks continually, which is often seen in scientific computing fields. The hard affinity can reduce the cost of switching between the cores. Some SFT systems with key units causing a large amount of computation is an example of such scenario. The developers can use the package *System.SFT_Elements* to give a hard affinity to such applications.

6. CONCLUSION

In this paper, we introduce the framework of multi-core based MOP and SFT, which can help programmers develop reliable software system. We propose the introduction of two new packages, *System.MOP_Elements* and *System.SFT_Elements*, which enable multi-core based MOP and SFT in Ada. Then we animate our proposal with a tool named MCAda. We use two case studies to show the implementation of multi-core based MOP and SFT in Ada. Meanwhile, the problem about the choice between hard affinity and soft affinity of tasks is discussed.

With the prevalence of multi-core platforms, our proposal can provide a better support for multi-core programming and reliable programming in Ada. The packages can hide the programming details of multi-core architectures and help the programmers who are unfamiliar with multi-core programming develop MOP and SFT systems in multi-core architectures. With these packages, programmers can migrate MOP and SFT systems to different multi-core platform with different physical cores. In addition, our proposal increases the readablity and undestandablity of MOP and SFT systems.

7. REFERENCES

[1] A. Avizienis. The methodology of n-version programming. In M. R. Lyu, editor, *SOFTWARE FAULT TOLERANCE*. John Wiley & Sons Ltd, 1994.

[2] P. G. Bishop. Software fault tolerance by design diversity. In *SOFTWARE FAULT TOLERANCE*, pages 211–229. John Wiley & Sons Ltd, 1994.

[3] F. Chen and G. Roşu. Mop: an efficient and generic runtime verification framework. In *OOPSLA '07: Proceedings of the 22nd annual ACM SIGPLAN conference on Object-oriented programming systems and applications*, pages 569–588, New York, NY, USA, 2007. ACM.

[4] M. B. Feldman. *Where is Ada used in Industry ?* http://www.seas.gwu.edu/ mfeldman/ada-project-summary.html, June,2008.

[5] J. C. Laprie, *et al*. Architectural issues in software fault tolerance. In M. R. Lyu, editor, *SOFTWARE FAULT TOLERANCE*, pages 47–80. John Wiley & Sons Ltd, 1994.

[6] Microsoft. *MSDN Library*. http://msdn2.microsoft.com/en-us/library/default.aspx.

[7] B. Randell and J. Xu. The evolution of the recovery block concept. In M. R. Lyu, editor, *SOFTWARE FAULT TOLERANCE*, pages 1–22. John Wiley & Sons Ltd, 1994.

[8] R. K. Scott, J. W. Gault, and D. F. McAllister. Fault-tolerant software reliability modeling. *IEEE Trans. Softw. Eng.*, 13(5):582–592, 1987.

[9] A. J. Wellings and A. Burns. Beyond ada 2005: allocating tasks to processors in smp systems. *Ada Lett.*, XXVII(2):75–81, 2007.

[10] L. Yang, Z. Cui, and X. Li. A case study for fault tolerance oriented programming in multi-core architecture. *High Performance Computing and Communications, 10th IEEE International Conference on*, 0:630–635, 2009.

[11] L. Yang, J. Tang, J. Zhao, and X. Li. A case study for monitoring-oriented programming in multi-core architecture. In *IWMSE '08: Proceedings of the 1st international workshop on Multicore software engineering*, pages 47–52, New York, NY, USA, 2008. ACM.

[12] L. Yang, L. Yu, J. Tang, L. Wang, J. Zhao, and X. Li. Enabling multi-core based monitoring and fault tolerance in c++/java. In *IWMSE '10: Proceedings of the 3rd International Workshop on Multicore Software Engineering*, pages 32–39, New York, NY, USA, 2010. ACM.

Towards Ada 2012: An Interim Report

Edmond Schonberg

Adacore Inc

104 5th Ave. NYC 10011

schonberg@gnat.com

ABSTRACT

The Ada Rapporteur Group (ARG), following the directives of ISO/IEC JTC1/SC22/WG9 is preparing an update to the Ada 2005 standard. This paper presents a snapshot of the more important language enhancements under discussion. Even though these enhancements are not yet in their final form, and will not become part of the proposed new standard until approved by ISO, the description that follows is an accurate reflection of the main directions in which the language is evolving. However, the names of packages, subprograms, and formal parameters, as well as some details of the syntax might change from what is presented here.

Categories and Subject Descriptors

D.3.3 [**Programming Languages**] Language Consructs and Features: abstract data types, control structures, modules, packages, concurrent programming structures

General Terms

Languages, standardization

Keywords

Ada, Ada 2005, Ada 2012

I INTRODUCTION

The WG9 committee, after discussions with the ARG and with members of the Ada community, has instructed the ARG to complete the Amendment to Ada 2005 [1] so that ISO standardization of the new version can be completed by 2012. This is a relatively short horizon, but it matches the interval between previous releases, demonstrates that the language continues to evolve, and at the same time places a bound on the changes to the language, and ensures that they do not present an undue implementation burden on existing compilers.

This paper is an informal survey of the more important enhancements that the ARG is discussing.[i] These enhancements are grouped as follows:

Section 2 discusses enhancements directly related to program correctness, namely the introduction of more powerful assertion mechanisms in the language: pre- and postconditions, type invariants, subtype predicates and other mechanisms that encourage the programmer to better specify the meaning of the

code they write, and allow the compiler and the run-time to verify that this meaning is in fact obeyed.

Section 3 discusses enhancements to the Containers library.

Section 4 presents language enhancements that contribute to expressiveness and readability: conditional expressions, case expressions, more powerful membership tests, and generalized iterator forms. Most of these are syntactic enhancements whose semantics is intuitive and fit well in Ada. One addition in this category has a larger import because it reverses an early design decision that had been controversial ever since Ada 83: functions will now have **in** and **in out** formal parameters.

Section 5 discusses visibility mechanisms: more powerful use clauses, and integrated packages that provide better access to declarations in nested packages.

Section 6 presents concurrency and real-time enhancements that address the multicore revolution.

Section 7 mentions other minor syntactic enhancements that simplify the programming task and polish some awkward corners of the language.

Each one of the enhancements we describe corresponds to one or more Ada Issues (AIs). We must emphasize that our descriptions are informal, and reflect the state of affairs as of this writing (August 2010). Please refer to the database at the Ada Information Clearinghouse (see www.ada-auth.org/AI05-SUMMARY.HTML where the interested reader will find up-to-date descriptions and a full list of Amendment AIs.

2 PROGRAM CORRECTNESS

The enhancements in this area address the familiar issue of "programming by contract" (see [2] for a modern discussion). They provide the programmer with tools to specify formally the intent of a construct. This formal description can then be verified/enforced at execution time, by means of assert statements that raise an exception if the stated intent is violated,. The specification can also be confirmed statically by analysis tools. Such contract specifications allow compilers and other tools to catch errors in usage or implementation earlier in the development cycle. They also provide valuable documentation of the intended semantics of an abstraction.

2.1 Aspect specifications   (AI05-0183)

Assertions about the behavior of subprograms, types, and objects are aspects of the corresponding entities, and a uniform syntax will be available to specify these, as well as more familiar operational and representational attributes of various kinds of entities. Thus the notion of aspect generalizes the familiar Ada concept of attribute. The properties of familiar attributes can be specified with representation clauses (for example size representation clauses) or with pragmas (for example pragma Pack). These specifications are now unified with the new notion of *aspect*:

```
aspect_specification ::=
    with aspect_mark [=> expression]
        {, aspect_mark [=> expression] }
```

An aspect specification can appear in object definitions, type declarations, all manner of subprogram declarations, component declarations and entry declarations. Specifiable aspects include among others size, alignment, packing, as well as the novel predicates described below.

2.2 Pre- and postconditions for subprograms (AI05-0145)

These aspects are predicates, that is to say boolean expressions that must be True on entry to (resp. on exit from) the subprogram to which they apply. The declaration of the function Pop for the canonical Stack data type might be given as follows:

```
function Pop (S : in out Stack) return Elem
    with
    Pre  => not Is_Empty(S),
    Post => not Is_Full(S);
```

A postcondition often needs to refer to the incoming value of an **in out** parameter or the value that a global object has before the subprogram is executed. The attribute 'Old, applied to any nonlimited entity, denotes its value on entry to the subprogram. Similarly, the attribute 'Result denotes the value returned by a function.

2.3 Type invariants (AI05-0146)

From a contractual point of view, the visible behavior of a private type is described indirectly through the pre- and postconditions that apply to the primitive operations of the type. Other contractual details of an abstraction are better described directly as properties of the type itself.

The new aspect notation allows us to write:

```
type T (...) is private
    with Type_Invariant => Is_Valid (T);

type T2 (...) is abstract tagged private
    with
       Type_Invariant'Class =>  Is_Valid (T2);

function Is_Valid (X : T) return Boolean;
```

Note that Is_Valid is referenced before its declaration. This may seem like a break from the Ada canonical linear order of elaboration, but in fact it corresponds to the rule that aspects are elaborated at the point the entity to which they apply is frozen (this is the point at which all the characteristics of the type must be known). In most cases this means the end of the enclosing library package declaration. This rule applies to all aspect specifications.

A type invariant can be type-specific, or class-wide, in which case it applies to all extensions of the type. An invariant is checked on exit from any visible subprogram that is a primitive operation of the type, including stream operations.

2.4 Subtype predicates (IA05-0153)

In addition to type invariants, it is often useful to specify properties of the values of a subtype which is not necessarily private. Most commonly the predicate mentions a scalar type, or a scalar component of a composite type:

```
type Rec is record
   A : Natural;
 end record;
 subtype Decimal_Rec is Rec
     with Subtype_Predicate =>
                   Rec.A mod 10 = 0;
```

A subtype predicate provides a solution to the common need to specify a non-contiguous subset of values of a scalar type. More powerful predicates may involve bounds, discriminants and other components.

3. CONTAINERS

Container libraries have become ubiquitous in modern programming environments. The enhancements in this area provide abstractions with better storage properties, task-safety, and useful search properties. There is one common advantage of standardized containers that is worth emphasizing: memory management of collections of values is handled by the container operations, not directly by the user. Storage allocation and reclamation are behind the scene, thus freeing the programmer from some of the more delicate and error-prone aspects of low-level programming. This is particularly important when indefinite types, such as class-wide types, are involved.

3.1 Bounded containers (AI05-0001)

In their more general form containers place objects and auxiliary data structures in the heap. Even though most heap management is hidden from the programmer, thanks to the use of controlled types, such heap usage is forbidden in high-integrity environments, which renders 2005 containers virtually useless in this realm of application. Ada 2012 introduces bounded variants of containers (vectors, lists, maps) that have a fixed capacity and so can be stack-allocated. The new container types are all discriminated types, constrained by capacity. The bounded containers are not themselves controlled types, which allows for a lighter implementation. (Of course, if the element type of a bounded container is controlled, the container itself will have to be finalized.)

This AI also adds to the Ada library several general purpose packages for case-insensitive operations on strings for sorting and for hashing.

3.2 Holder containers (AI05-0069)

In Ada 2005 it is not possible to declare a variable of an indefinite type without giving it an initial value that fixes its constraints once and for all. The holder container is a wrapper that can hold a single value of some (possibly indefinite) type. This value can be queried and modified, thus providing the equivalent of a variable of an indefinite type. The generic package has a formal type with unknown discriminants, and a formal equality operation. Such a container is often called a Singleton in other languages.

3.3 Synchronized queues (AI05-0159)

Queues were omitted from the 2005 Container library, because they were considered trivial to write, and too elementary to be included in a language standard. However, Queues that are task-safe are somewhat more complex, and it is worthwhile to standardize an efficient version of such shared data-structures. Ada 2012 introduces a package Ada.Containers.Synchronized_Queues.Interfaces, that declares a synchronized interface with abstract queue operations, and several packages that implement that interface and export a protected type Queue:

Bounded_Synchronized_Queues
Unbounded_Synchronized_Queues
Bounded_Priority_Queues
Unbounded_Priority_Queues

Each one of these packages is parameterized by an instantiation of Synchronized_Queues that specifies the element type. In addition, the resulting type Queue is discriminated by its ceiling priority. For example:

```
with Ada.Containers.Synchronized_Queue.Interfaces;
generic
    with package Queue_Interfaces is new
        Ada.Containers.Synchronized_Queue_Interfaces (<>);
        Default_Ceiling : System.Any_Priority := System.Priority'Last;
package Ada.Containers.Unbounded_Synchronized_Queues is
    pragma Preelaborate;

    protected type Queue (Ceiling : System.Any_Priority := Default_Ceiling) is
    new Queue_Interfaces.Queue with
        entry Enqueue(New_Item: Queue_Interfaces.Element_Type);
    …  other queue operations
private
        -- not specified by the language
    end Ada.Containers.Unbounded_Synchronized_Queues;
```

Similar generic units are provided for bounded queues and for the priority queue variants

The final structure of the queue packages is not finalized. Some further flexibility is needed to describe the private part of the protected object that actually manages the queue itself. The complicating issue is that it would be preferable to make that type private, but this would force the protected type itself to be placed in the private part.

3.4 Multiway trees (AI05-0136)

Trees are the quintessential dynamic data structures, and ones for which hiding storage management activities in the implementation is particularly worthwhile. The Container library will now include a very general tree structure, a multiway tree, where each internal node has a vector of descendant nodes, so that there is easy navigation from a node to its siblings and to its ancestors. Search and insertion operations on this structure must have a complexity of O (Log (N)).

4. FUNCTIONS, EXPRESSIONS, CONTROL STRUCTURES

The enhancements in this group aim to simplify programming in the small: more expressive function declarations, new expression forms, better notation for existing constructs. Most of these can be considered syntactic sugar, that is to say shortcuts to common program fragments that can be written in today's Ada. These forms are also useful for expressing complex pre/post conditions and other contract predicates. The first enhancement in this group, however, has a deeper semantic impact.

4.1 In out parameters for functions (AI05-0143)

Ever since Ada 83, functions have had only **in** parameters, with the (always controversial) justification that they were intended to be the equivalent of mathematical (pure) functions with no side effects. However functions can modify global variables and call procedures that do, and thus have arbitrary side effects for which there is no syntactic indication. In Ada 2012, functions will have both **out** and **in out** parameters, to indicate more explicitly the way in which a function call may affect the state of the program.

4.2 Dangerous order dependences (AI05-0144)

This in turn highlights a weakness in the way Ada specifies (or fails to specify) the order of evaluation of expressions and parameters in calls. If functions have **in out** parameters, there is a greater danger that side effects will make the evaluation of an expression non-deterministic. To alleviate the problem, Ada 2012 mandates static checks that make many common order-dependences illegal. For example, if F is a function with an **in out** parameter, the expression:

$$F (Obj) + G (Obj)$$

has an illegal order-dependence because the result may be different depending on the order in which the operands of this expression are evaluated. Similarly, the new rules force a compiler to reject aliasing between two actual parameters of an elementary type, when one of the formals is not an **in** parameter. The checks mandated by AI05-0144 can be made linear in the size of the expression involved (call or assignment). These checks depend on a static definition of when two names denote the same object, or when one name denotes a portion of the object denoted by the other. Unlike more rigorous verification systems such as Spark [3], the checks proposed by this AI cannot be complete, given that arbitrary side effects may be present through global variables or access types; they do nevertheless eliminate the most egregious examples of order-dependences.

Ada will remain free of idioms that rely on a particular order of evaluation, such as the celebrated C idiom for copying strings:

```
(while *p++ = *q++);
```

A related proposal, AI05-0191, describes explicit aliasing predicates to indicate that two objects overlap in full or in part. Programming such predicates turns out to be very delicate, but it is easier for a compiler to generate the code needed to verify them.

4.3 Conditional and case expressions (AI05-0147 and AI05-0188)

The chief purpose of these syntactic shortcuts (familiar from other programming languages, such as C++ and various functional languages) is to simplify writing pre- and postconditions, as well as type invariants. These are often complex predicates which would have to be written as off-line functions, thus making them more opaque. Conditional and case expressions allow these predicates to be directly attached to the declaration of the entity to which they apply:

```
procedure Append
  (V : Vector; To : Vector)
  with Pre =>
  (if Size (V) > 0 then
      Capacity (To) > Size (V)
   else True);
```

It is frequently the case that predicates impose a check in one case but not in the other, so the trailing else True can be omitted in that case:

```
procedure Append
  (V : Vector; To : Vector)
  with Pre =>
  (if Size (V) > 0 then
      Capacity (To) > Size (V));
```

Conditional expressions can also be useful to simplify existing code involving if_ statements, though here tastes may differ. For example, there might be a definite advantage in rewriting an if_statement if both of its branches contain two subprogram calls that differ only in one actual parameter, e.g.:

```
Eval (X + Y, F(if Cond then 1 else 0));
```

instead of

```
if Cond then
    Eval (X + Y, F (1));
else
    Eval (X + Y, F (0));
end if;
```

The semantics of conditional expressions is identical to that of short-circuit expressions. Conditional expressions are static if the condition and both dependent expressions are static.

Case expressions stand in the same relation to case statements as conditional expressions to if statements. The well-understood advantage of case expressions is that the compiler can verify that all cases are covered. Thus a case expression is safer than a conditional expression with a series of tests.

4.4 Parameterized Expressions (AI05-0177)

We can anticipate that the use of pre- and postconditions will encourage software designers to write more complex expressions to describe behavior. It is well-known that complex Boolean expressions are notoriously error-prone. Thus the proposal to provide a syntax for function bodies that can appear directly in a package declaration, and can be invoked in pre/post conditions and invariants. Such function expressions provide the author of the code with a useful abstraction, and the client with a better indication of intended usage, than if the body of the function were relegated to a package body.

4.5 Iterators, Accessors, and References (AI05-0139)

Traversing a collection is an extremely common programming idiom. If the collection is described by one of the library containers, iteration over it can be described by means of the primitive operations First and Next. These operations typically use cursors to provide access to elements in the collection. However, it is often clearer to refer directly to the elements of the collection, without the indirection implied by the presence of the cursor. This AI will make it possible to write, for example:

```
for Cur in Iterate (My_Coll) loop
    My_Coll (Cur) := My_Coll (Cur) + 1;
end loop;
```

as well as:

```
for Element of My_coll loop
    Element := Element + 1;
end loop;
```

This syntactic extension is obtained by means of a predefined limited interface Reference, whose built-in characteristic is that it has an access discriminant that denotes an element of a container, and that any reference to an object that implements the interface is an implicit dereference of the discriminant. Thus, if Ref_T is a type that implemntes Reference, and Element is a primitive operation of some type Table that returns a Ref_T, then Tab.Element (Some_Key) is implicitly a cursor into Tab, and can be used either to retrieve or modify the corresponding element of the container, This allows us to treat arbitrary containers (in particular sets and maps) as if they were indexable structures.

To complete this scheme, two new aspects are introduced: Constant_Indexing and Variable_Indexing, whose value must be a primitive operation of a container (or more generally some limited composite type) that returns a Reference. The use of one of these functions yields a constant or a variable view of an element of the container.

Finally, a predefined package Ada.Iterator_Interfaces makes use of these aspects to define Forward and backward Iterators over containers.

An instantiation of this package is present in every predefined container, but the user can instantiate such a generic and provide special-purpose First and Next functions to perform partial iterations and iterations in whatever order is convenient. The familiar keyword **reverse** can be used to determine the direction of iteration.

4.6 Extended membership operations (AI05-0158)

The current machinery to define subtypes has no provision for declaring a subset of the values of a scalar type that is not contiguous. Membership in such a subset must be expressed as a series of tests:

```
type Color is

(Red, Green, Blue,Cyan, Magenta, Yellow);

 Hue : Color;
    ...
  if Hue = Red or else Hue = Blue
     or else Hue = Yellow then ...
```

The proposed enhanced membership notation allows sequences of values to appear as the right operand:

```
  if Hue in (Red |   Blue | Yellow ) then
...
```

Once this notation is introduced, it can be extended to any non-limited type:

```
if Name in
 ("Entry" | "Exit" | Dict("Urgence")
then ...
```

This notation can then be used to declare subtype predicates as well.

4.7 Quantified expressions (AI05-0176)

Invariants declared over containers are often expressed as predicates over all the elements of the container. The familiar notation of Set Theory provides the model for introducing quantified expressions into Ada:

```
Quantified_Expression ::=
             Quantifier Iterator  "|" Predicate

Quantifier  ::=  for all | for some
Iterator    ::=  defining_identifier in expression
Predicate   ::=  Boolean_expression
```

The vertical bar is usually read as "such that" or "it is the case that".

For example, a postcondition on a sorting routine might be written as:

```
for all J in
     A'First .. Index'Pred (A'Last)
     | A (J) <= A (Index'Succ (J));
```

We have departed from the standard notation and rejected the use of *exists* as a new keyword, because it is in common use in much installed software. Instead, the new reserved word **some** (the only new one in Ada 2012), appearing after keyword **for**, specifies that the expression is existentially quantified. For example, the predicate Is_Composite applied to some positive integer might be (inefficiently) described thus:

```
(for some J in 2 .. N/2 | N mod J = 0)
```

The iterator forms proposed in AI05-0139 will also be usable in quantified expressions.

5. VISIBILITY

The Ada Issues in this category aim to simplify the programming task by providing simpler ways for names to denote specific entities, and by allowing wider uses for entities of certain kinds.

5.1 Use all type (AI05-0150)

The Ada community has been divided over the presence of use clauses ever since Ada 83. Certain style guides forbid use clauses altogether, which forces programmers to qualify all names imported from another unit. To lighten this rather heavy burden, which among other things forces the use of the awkward notation P."+", the use_type clause introduced in Ada 95 provides use-visibility to the operators of a type defined in another unit, so that infix notation (X + Y) is legal even when the type of X and Y is not use-visible. AI05-0150 extends this visibility to all primitive operations of a type (including the literals of an enumeration type). If the type is tagged, this is extended as well to subprograms that operate on T'Class, subprograms that may be declared in packages containing ancestors of type T.

5.2 Issues of nested instantiations (AI05-0135 and others)

It is common for a library package P to contain an instantiation of some other package Inner, in order to export a type T declared within Inner. This is often done by means of a derived type DT, which inherits the operations of T and makes them available to a client of P. However, this derivation is a programming artifact (in the vernacular, a kludge) and it is desirable to find a more direct way of re-exporting the entities declared in an inner package. A related issue is that of private instantiations: a package declares a private type PT and needs to declare a container of objects of this type. The instantiation cannot appear in the same package before the full declaration for PT, which leads to a contorted architecture. The ARG is examining several proposals to simplify these programming patterns, including integrated packages (whose contents are immediately visible in the enclosing package) and formal incomplete types for generic units.

5.3 Incomplete types completed by partial views (AI05-0162)

In many situations we declare an incomplete type in order to provide an access type used in some other construct. The completion of the incomplete type must occur within the same declarative part. For purposes of information hiding, we may want to complete the incomplete declaration with a private type, but this is currently forbidden by the language. This AI proposes that the completion of an incomplete type declaration may be any type declaration (except another incomplete one). Type declarations can thus be given in three parts: an incomplete type declaration, a private type declaration, and finally a full type declaration.

5.4 Incomplete parameter and result types (AI05-0151)

Limited with_clauses make it possible to describe mutually recursive types declared in separate packages, by providing incomplete views of types. If such an incomplete view is tagged, then it can be used as the formal in a subprogram declaration and even in a call, because objects of the type are known to be passed by reference. This AI extends the use of untagged incomplete types obtained through limited views, so they can be used as well as parameter types and result types, as long as the full view of the type is available at a point of call. For tagged types, it is possible to use them as well in the profile of bodies and in calls, because of their reference semantics.

6. CONCURRENCY AND REAL TIME

Most programming languages are proposing new constructs to make proper use of the multicore chips that will dominate the hardware landscape of the next decade. The International Real-Time Ada Workshop has proposed a number of language extensions to simplify the programming of such architectures [4].

6.1 Affinities   (AI05-0167)

The first requirement is a mechanism to describe the set of available processing cores in a chip, and to specify a mapping (partitioning) between tasks and cores. In existing operating systems, this mapping is often described as the "affinity" of the task, and the control of task affinities in multiprocessor systems is as important as the control of priorities. This is achieved by means two child packages of System:

a) System.Multiprocessors describes the underlying hardware as an array of processors.

b) System.Multiprocessors.Dispatching_Domains allows the user to specify subranges of the full set array of processors, and assign individual tasks to a given dispatching domain. Each domain has its own ready queue, and possibly a distinct scheduling policy. It is possible for a task to determine which CPU it is currently executing on.

Needless to say, the implementation of these operations depends on the availability of lower-level constructs in the underlying operating system. The paper by Saez and Crespo [5] indicates that at least on GNU-Linux operating systems their implementation is relatively straightforward today.

6.2 Extending the Ravenscar Profile to multiprocessor systems (AI05-0171)

The Ravenscar profile [6] has been extremely successful for real-time applications, and is in wide use today. This AI proposes its extension to multi-processor systems, to facilitate the construction of deterministic and analyzable tasking programs that can be supported with a run-time system of reduced size and complexity. The proposed extensions to the Ravenscar profile depend on the partitioning facilities described above, but forbid dynamic task migration and require that a task be on the ready queue of a single processor. This excludes the use of dispatching domains in Ravenscar.

6.3 Barriers   (AI05-0174)

Barriers are basic synchronization primitives that were originally motivated by loop parallelism. Operating systems such as POSIX already provide barriers, where a set of tasks is made to wait until a specified number of them are ready to proceed, at which time all of them are released. The effect of a barrier can be simulated with a protected type, but only with substantial overhead and potential serialization, so a new mechanism is needed. This mechanism is provided by means of a new package: Ada.Synchronous_Barriers, that exports a positive subtype Barrier_Limit, and a limited type Synchronous_Barrier, with a

discriminant Number_Waiting of this numeric type. The basic operation provided on barrier is a procedure Wait_For_Release:

```
procedure Wait_For_Release
  (The_Barrier :
           in out Synchronous_Barrier;;
   Notified : out Boolean);
```

When a variable of type Barrier is created with Number_Waiting = N, there are no waiting tasks and the barrier is set to block tasks whenever they invoke Wait_For_Release. When the count reaches N, all tasks are simultaneously released and the **out** parameter Notified is set in an arbitrary one of the callers, which then performs cleanup actions for the whole set. Note that this is different from the Ada 2005 proxy model for a protected operation: there the task that modifies the barrier executes sequentially, in some unspecified order, the pending actions of all tasks queued on the barrier.

This construct is intented for straightforward loop-parallelism, and its use in the presence of asynchronous transfer of control or abort statements is in general erroneous.

6.4 Requeue on Synchronized interfaces (AI05-0030)

The introduction of synchronized interfaces is one of the most attractive innovations of Ada 2005: a concurrent construct may be implemented by means of an active entity (a task) or a passive one (a protected object), both of which may include queues to enforce mutual exclusion.   However, only functions and procedures are allowed as primitive operations of interfaces. It is desirable to support the construction of concurrent algorithms that involve requeue statements, where the construct on which the requeue is to take place may be either a task or a protected object. This AI proposes a pragma to indicate that a given interface operation may allow requeuing:

```
procedure Q(S : in out Server; X :Item);
```

```
pragma Implemented (Q, By_Entry);
```

The   pragma   can   also   take   the   parameters By_Protected_Procedure and By_Any.

7. SYNTACTIC FRILLS

The AIs in this category address small programming irritants in the syntax of the language, and simplify the programming of common idioms.

7.1 Labels count as statements (AI05-0179)

One of the most common uses of gotos in Ada is to provide the equivalent of a "continue" statement in a loop, namely to skip part of the body of the loop and start the next iteration. The following pattern will be familiar:

```
loop
   ...
   if Cond then goto Continue; end if;
   ...
   <<Continue>> null;
end loop;
```

The null statement is only noise, forced by the current rule that a label is part of a statement. The rule proposed in this AI is that a label by itself is a valid constituent of a statement sequence. This simple rule was chosen, instead of the more contentious introduction of a new reserved word *continue* to be used as a new statement form.

7.2 Pragmas instead of null (AI05-0163)

Programmers have found the current rules for pragma placement confusing and error-prone. The syntactic rules concerning them have been simplified, so that they can appear in an otherwise empty sequence of statements, without requiring the presence of an explicit null statement to make the sequence legal.

8. CONCLUSIONS

The Ada 2012 amendment strikes a balance between conflicting requirements:

- On the one hand, the evolution of software engineering suggests new language features to facilitate the construction of ever-more-complex systems.

- On the other hand, the large established software base mandates that all new constructs be upward compatible, easy to describe and relatively easy to implement.

- Finally, the Ada community expects the language to evolve, reflecting the development of software methodologies and the evolution of other languages in the same domain.

Time will tell how well the proposed amendment navigates between these constraints. Some partial implementations of the new features are appearing in existing compilers, which will allow language enthusiasts to experiment with them early on. We trust that the Ada community will welcome the new face of the language.

9. ACKNOWLEDGMENTS

This paper summarizes the collective work of the ARG. The contributions of three of its members over the years deserve special mention: Randy Bruckardt (editor in chief) John Barnes (explainer in chief) and Tucker Taft (designer in chief). Remaining errors and omissions are the author's sole responsibility.

10. REFERENCES

[1] Tucker Taft, S., Duff, R.A., Brukardt, R.L, Ploedereder, E., Leroy, P.: Ada Reference Manual, LNCS, vol, 4348, Springer, Heidelberg (2006)

[2] Fowler, M.: UML distilled, Third Edition, Pearson Education, Boston, MA (2004)

[3] Barnes, J.: High Integrity Software; The SPARK approach to Safety and Security, Pearson Education, Boston MA (2003)

[4] Special issue of Ada Letters on the proceedings of IRTAW-14, Porto Venere, Italy, 2009 (in press)

[5] Sergio Saez and Alfonso Crespo: Preliminary Support of Ada2012 in GNU/Linux systems: Ada-Europe 2010, LNCS)

[6] Burns, A., Dobbing, B., Vardanega, T.: Guide for the use of the Ada Ravenscar Profile in High Integrity Systems. Ada Lett. XXIV (2), 1-74 (2004)

---

[i] A preliminary version of this paper was presented at Ada-Europe 2010, Valencia, Spain, June 16 2010

The Rise, Fall and Persistence of Ada

Ricky E. Sward
MITRE Corporation
1155 Academy Park Loop, Colorado Springs, CO 80910
1-719-572-8263
rsward@mitre.org

ABSTRACT

This paper begins with a brief history of the Ada programming language including the rise of Ada, the Ada Mandate and the fall from grace as a DoD programming language. The paper examines the reasons why the Ada is not widely accepted in certain areas and provides reasons why it should be used in particular areas. The paper then gives examples of where Ada has persisted and found a niche in safety critical, high integrity. The paper also discusses Ada-related organizations and gives examples of projects currently underway in the US and in Europe providing a compelling reason for using Ada in appropriate and critical domain areas.

Categories and Subject Descriptors

D.2.0 [**Software**]: Software Engineering – *General*

General Terms: Design, Languages

Keywords: Ada Programming Language, History of Ada, Safety Critical, High Integrity.

1. Introduction

The Ada programming language has experienced an incredible history of widely accepted use, a fall from grace and a recent resurgence in the area of high integrity, safety critical systems. Currently, Ada is not widely accepted as a programming language, but there is a compelling case for why its strengths are very applicable in particular domains. Ada is the correct choice as a programming language in these domains.

The paper begins with a history of Ada in the early days and continues through the Ada Mandate and its removal in 1997. The paper then describes the recent trends towards using Ada in safety critical, high integrity systems. Several organizations are still active in the area of Ada programming and the paper gives details on these organizations. Finally, the paper discusses several large, recent projects that are using the Ada programming language.

2. The History of Ada

In the 1970s, the Department of Defense (DoD) embarked on a

MITRE Public Release Approval 10-3151.

historic project to develop a programming language that could be used on every DoD programming project. The intent was to design a modular programming language that could be used on embedded computer system projects. By 1980, MIL-STD-1815 was published and in 1983 the ANSI standard was published [1]. Ada 83 was the first standardized version of Ada.

2.1 The Rise of Ada

Ada 83 gained wide public attention and acceptance during what is called 'the early days' or 'heydays of Ada'. Some thought that Ada could become a dominant general purpose programming language and not just used for embedded systems on DoD projects. The language was designed with three very appealing goals in mind: program reliability and maintenance, programming as a human activity, and efficiency [2]. But in part due to these ambitious goals, early compilers struggled to implement Ada 83. The compilers that were developed were large, cumbersome and expensive.

Ada includes the use of strong typing, modular design, parallel processing, exception handling and generics which are appealing aspects of the language [1]. Ada includes run-time checks to avoid common programming errors such as off-by-one errors, array access errors, and access to unallocated memory. Ada also includes compile time checks that finds errors that would not be detected until runtime in other popular programming languages [1]. These features made Ada an appealing and effective language for DoD embedded real-time systems which may cause loss of life if an error occurs during execution of the program.

In 1987, the DoD established the Ada Mandate requiring Ada to be used on all DoD software system projects. However, waivers for not using Ada on software systems were often given during this timeframe. Ada compilers improved in performance and capability, but still struggled to implement the full capabilities of the language [1].

2.2 The Fall of Ada

By 1997, the DoD did not require Ada to be used in new DoD software projects and effectively removed the Ada Mandate. The DoD leadership had been ineffective in enforcing the Ada Mandate between 1987 and 1997 because waivers for not using Ada had been granted on the majority of DoD software projects.

Ada had been declining in usage and popularity by 1997 in part due to the Ada Mandate itself. Given the nature of software engineers, they were not enamored with the idea of being told what programming language to use to develop their software. Other popular programming languages at the time included C++ and Java.

Ada had also been declining in usage and popularity in part due to the lack of effective compilers. The existing compilers added to the frustration of software engineers because the compilers were slow and expensive. Not only were the software engineers being told what language to use, but they were being told to use slow, ineffective tools to develop their software.

Although the language features were appealing and the Ada 1995 version included support of object-oriented programming (OOP), the political and social forces of the time caused the decline and fall from favor of Ada. This fall from grace has remained to this day even though it has been 13 years since the Ada Mandate was removed.

Those involved with Ada often get responses such as "Is Ada still around?" or "I didn't know people still use Ada." from people they talk to. These responses are often accompanied with smiles or a laugh. It seems that the mention of using Ada for a software engineering project brings back memories of the Ada Mandate and the fall from grace, which may be the only thing they remember about Ada. It's ironic that the Ada Mandate and the fall from grace have had such a long lasting negative effect on the use of the Ada programming language. Even after 13 years, the language is not able to shake this stigma.

3. The Persistence of Ada

Despite its stigma, Ada has survived and is still being used on systems where it is appropriate. The original goals of Ada still apply to systems where a loss of life may occur, i.e. safety critical, high integrity systems. Ada has found a niche and strong foothold in organizations that develop these systems. The Ada language continues to be updated and improved to meet the needs of today's programmers.

3.1 Ada's Popularity Rating

An interesting statistic about Ada is that as of June 2010, it is ranked #26 on the list of popular programming languages [3]. This ranking from Tiobe is based on the number of skilled engineers world-wide, courses available for the language and the number of third party vendors [3]. Java, C and C++ are at the top of the rankings, but Ada is above other long-time languages such as COBOL and FORTRAN. Another interesting statistic from the Tiobe site is the long term history of the popularity of Ada.

Programming Language	Position Jun 2010	Position Jun 2005	Position Jun 1995	Position Jun 1985
Ada	26	18	6	3

Table 1 – Long Term Popularity of Ada [3]

As you can see from Table 1, the popularity of Ada in 1985 reflects the early days of Ada with only C and Lisp ranked above it [3]. Ada was still holding strong in 1995 and rated the 6th most popular programming language. By 2005, Ada had fallen from grace and was declining in popularity.

3.2 Why use Ada today?

Ada's original goals to provide program reliability and maintenance, to treat programming as a human activity, and to provide program efficiency have been successfully built into the language and improved on over the years. More than ever, Ada is a language that provides benefits for the software development organization. Large, complex software systems are often developed by one team of

software engineers and then, over the years, maintained by a different team. The initial development costs of building a software system in Ada are easily out-weighed by the benefits of correctness, reliability and maintainability in a large, complex, safety critical software system [1]. The language design principles of Ada can benefit most software development projects, but in the realm of safety critical systems, these benefits have become the clearest.

Recent versions of the Ada language still include strong typing, modular design, parallel processing, exception handling and generics which are appealing aspects of the language [1]. Recent versions of the language have added support for Object-Oriented Programming, a popular programming paradigm. There is also now support for using Ada in a Service Oriented Architecture (SOA), another recent programming paradigm [4].

Ada compilers have come a long way since the late 1990's. The Gnat Ada compiler is part of the GNU Compiler Collection [5] and is available for Windows, Unix, and Linux platforms.

3.3 Safety Critical, High Integrity Niche

Ada has clearly found a niche in developing software for safety critical, high integrity systems. Systems that may cause loss of life if an error occurs rely on the correctness and reliability of Ada. As a programming language design feature, Ada has been designed to detect small problems in very large software systems [1]. Software systems for avionics, air traffic control systems, and robotics are currently being developed using Ada.

Ada's support for a large number of compile-time and run-time checks protects the software system against common errors. Examples of these errors include the use of undeclared and uninitialized variables, assigning values outside the proper range of a variable or array, buffer overflow, unclear definition of code blocks, and procedure calls with incorrect parameters. All these error checks improve the quality and reliability of the software being developed. Ada's checks will cause a software engineer to spend more time getting the software to compile properly. But once the software compiles, the run-time errors will be limited to errors in logic versus errors in values assigned to variables or buffer overflows, etc.

Recently, there has also been support for program verification using a sub-set of the Ada programming language. The SPARK programming language [6] applies the principles of Correctness by Construction [7] to the development of software systems. SPARK has been specifically designed to support the development of safety critical, high integrity systems.

3.4 Use in Universities

As Ada went through its heyday in the early years and then the subsequent fall from grace, the programming language found its way into university classrooms. There were several textbooks available for using Ada in CS-1 and CS-2 course in a Computer Science curriculum [8]. Notable textbooks include the Programming in Ada series by John Barnes, the Ada Plus Data Structures text from Nell Dale and John McCormick, the Ada 95 Problem Solving and Program Design text from Mike Feldman, Introductory Problem Solving Using Ada 95 from Tim Chamillard and the Ada as a Second Language text from Norman Cohen.

Ada was taught as the introductory language for students at the US Air Force Academy (USAFA) and the US Military Academy

(USMA) for several years in the 1990's and 2000's. In 2003, the USAFA staff made a compelling argument for using Ada as their introductory language in the Computer Science major [9]. However, Ada is no longer taught at the USAFA as the introductory language. Ada is still being taught at the USMA as the introductory course. It is also used in robotics research by the faculty [10].

The AdaCore Corporation also hosts the GNAT Academic Program (GAP), which is dedicated to building a community of academic professionals using Ada in universities [11]. Currently the GAP community includes over 175 members in 35 countries teaching Ada using GNAT.

Ada is being taught at the University of Northern Iowa (UNI) and John McCormick published a compelling case study of students using C versus students using Ada in his real-time systems course [12]. For each comparison, students using Ada completed the assignment even though they were given very little support code from the instructor. The students using C did not complete the assignment even though they had been given large amounts of supporting code in the form of libraries from their instructor.

3.5 Ada Language Updates

Since the first ANSI and ISO standards established Ada 83, the Ada programming language has continued to be updated and improved. In 1995, the joint ISO/ANSI standard (ISO-8652:1995) was published adding support for polymorphism, hierarchical libraries, protected objects, predefined libraries, and specialized annexes to the Ada programming language [18]. An amendment to the language standard was made in 2007 establishing Ada 2005. This version improved the object-oriented syntax, enhanced structure and visibility control, and made improvements to tasking, exceptions, generics, and numerics [18]. There is also currently work going on to make another amendment to the Ada standard with a completion date targeted at 2012.

4. Ada Organizations

There are several organizations that are involved with the Ada programming language including American and European organizations. There is also a consortium of corporations that are also involved with Ada and organizations responsible for the ISO standard for Ada. The intent of this section of the paper is to show current activities and organizations involved in Ada.

4.1 SIGAda

The Association for Computing Machinery (ACM) Special Interest Group on Ada (SIGAda) is an American organization that brings together practitioners, educators and researchers working in the area of Ada. The membership for SIGAda has been near 300 for the last five years. SIGAda continues to hold an annual conference at different locations around the United States.

In March 2010, SIGAda went through a viability assessment by the ACM and was renewed for another four years. The review examined the finances, membership and goals of the organization. ACM agrees that SIGAda continues to provide a benefit to the community and its membership through the annual conference, the Ada Letters Journal, and its support for new versions of Ada and language standardization.

4.2 Ada Europe

Ada Europe is an international organization that has been set up to promote the use of Ada in Europe [14]. It consists of a consortium of member organizations from Belgium, Denmark, Germany, France, Spain, Sweden and Switzerland. Ada Europe is the sister organization of SIGAda and has a reciprocal agreement to send delegates from Ada Europe to the SIGAda annual conference and vice versa. Ada Europe includes around 300 members from all membership categories.

Ada Europe is best known for its annual conference held at different locations in Europe each year. The acceptance rate for this conference, named the Reliable Software Technologies Conference, is usually around 35% and is very selective. The conference includes three days of paper presentations and two days of tutorials on Ada and related topics.

Ada Europe also produces the Ada User's Journal on a quarterly basis. This journal includes Ada-related papers, experience reports and information on upcoming Ada-related events.

4.3 Ada Resource Association

The Ada Resource Association (ARA) is a group of Ada related companies dedicated to the continued use of Ada and to the support of Ada users. The mission of the ARA is "To ensure continued success of Ada users and promote Ada use in the software industry" [14]. The ARA supports Ada activities such as Ada-related conferences.

4.4 WG9 and the ARG

Since becoming an ANSI and MIL-STD in 1983 and then being adopted by the ISO in 1987, work has continued to improve the technical content of Ada. The WG9 is a working group under the ISO that is responsible for standards related to the Ada programming language. The Ada Rapporteur Group (ARG) is charged with handling comments on the Ada language standard. The ARG then reports to the WG9 working group on suggested technical improvements and changes to the language.

5. Ada Projects

This section of the paper gives examples of projects currently using the Ada programming language.

5.1 ERAM and Next Gen

Lockheed Martin is currently working on the En Route Automation Modernization (ERAM) system using the Ada programming language. The new ERAM system will replace the computer system that has been in place since 1967, which is called the HOST Computer System.

> "The ERAM system will provide a modular, expandable and supportable infrastructure that can accommodate innovation and steady enhancements. Considered an integral part of the Next Generation Air Transportation System (NextGen), the ERAM system is scheduled for deployment by 2010 at all 20 U.S. FAA En Route Air Route Traffic Control Centers (ARTCCs)." [15]

The FAA's NextGen project is overhauling our national airspace with the intent of making air travel less expensive and more convenient. ERAM is an integral part of the NextGen project.

5.2 The Boeing 777

The new Boeing 777 aircraft is currently flying with 99% of its software written in Ada. This includes the primary flight control systems, the braking systems, and the electrical power sub-system [16]. The teams built over 600K lines of Ada code for the primary flight control systems involving over 500 software engineers [16]. Ada's strong typing and modular design features allowed the software implementation to be split amongst large teams of 60-100 engineers. The integration of these components of the system then went very well due to the strict interface rules that can be enforced by Ada at compile time. The high level of accuracy during compile time meant less time spent debugging errors at run time [16].

5.3 European Air Traffic Control

The United Kingdom has decided to use SPARK to develop their next generation Air Traffic Control (ATC) system called the Interim Future Area Control Tools Support (iFACTS) [17]. The Praxis corporation was selected as the prime contractor for this new ATC system. The new iFACTS system will be a major part of Britain's National Air Traffic Services (NATS), which provides ATC services at their biggest airports. NATS also provides ATC support for aircraft flying en-route through the UK airspace.

5.4 MITRE robotics

The MITRE Corporation has been using Ada in robotics projects for several years. In 2005, the MITRE Meteor robotic truck competed in the DARPA grand challenge. The Meteor successfully traversed a full sized obstacle course using only computer vision and artificial intelligence decision making [19]. The Meteor competed in the semi-final event of the DARPA grand challenge. The Meteor's control systems are written in Ada using the RTEMS real-time executive for embedded systems [20].

5.5 Tokeneer

Ada has also been used in security related projects. The intent of the Tokeneer project was to show that a software system could be developed to meet the rigor of the higher assurance levels of the Common Criteria [20]. These levels of security assurance require formal proofs of program correctness. Praxis used formal methods for requirements specification, design and verification of program correctness. They used SPARK Ada to implement the system. Ada's features lend themselves well to development of security systems and can attain high levels of assurance as shown with the Tokeneer project.

6. Conclusions

The purpose of this paper is to show that while not a widely used programming language, Ada has found a niche in the development of certain types of software systems. There are several features of Ada that make it appealing for high integrity, safety critical systems as well as large scale, complex systems. Since the end of the Ada Mandate in 1997, Ada has declined in usage, but persists in these domains. Updates and improvements continue to be made to the language with new versions in 1995, 2005 and 2012. Several projects continue to use Ada as the primary development language.

Ada may never become a widely accepted, mainstream development language, but its features continue to be appealing to software developers in certain domains. Software engineers should understand that Ada is not a dead, unused language, but is instead a powerful language that is being applied in appropriate domains to complex software engineering problems.

7. References

[1] Ada Programming Language. Retrieved from http://en.wikipedia.org/wiki/Ada_(programming_language)

[2] Ada Language Reference Manual. LRM-2005.

[3] Tiobe Programming Language Ranking for June 2010. Retrieved from http://www.tiobe.com/index.php/content/paperinfo/tpci/index.html

[4] Sward, Ricky E. *Using Ada in a service-oriented architecture.* Proceedings of the 2007 ACM SIGAda international conference on Ada. Fairfax, Virginia, USA

[5] GNU Compiler Collection (GCC). Retrieved from http://en.wikipedia.org/wiki/GNU_Compiler_Collection

[6] The SPARK Programming Language, Retrieved from http://www.altran-praxis.com/spark.aspx

[7] Anthony Hall and Roderick Chapman. *Correctness by Construction: Developing a Commercial Secure System*, IEEE Software Jan/Feb 2002, pp18-25.

[8] List of Ada Textbooks. Retrieved from http://www.adaic.org/learn/textbook.html

[9] Sward, Ricky E. and Martin Carlisle, Barry Fagin, David Gibson. *The case for Ada at the USAF Academy.* Proceedings of the 2003 annual ACM SIGAda international conference on Ada. San Diego, CA.

[10] A Robotics API Dialect for Type-Safe Robots: Translating Myro to Ada. A. S. Mentis. Proceedings of the 2009 annual ACM SIGAda international conference on Ada. Tampa Bay, FL.

[11] GNAT Academic Program (GAP). Retrieved from http://www.adacore.com/home/academia/

[12] McCormick, John. *Ada and software engineering education: one professor's experiences.* Proceedings of the 2007 annual ACM SIGAda international conference on Ada. Portland, OR.

[13] Ada Europe. Retrieved from http://www.ada-europe.org

[14] Ada Resource Association. Retrieved from http://www.adaic.org/ARA/index.html

[15] ERAM. Retrieved from http://www.lockheedmartin.com/news/press_releases/2007/1010ts_FAAEnRouteAutomation.html

[16] Boeing 777. Retrieved from http://www.adaic.org/atwork/boeing.html

[17] iFACTS. Retrieved from http://www.drdobbs.com/embedded-systems/199905389

[18] Ada2005 Language Rationale. Retrieved from http://www.adaic.org/standards/05rat/html/Rat-TOC.html

[19] MITRE Meteor. Retrieved from http://www.mitre.org/tech/meteor/

[20] C. Cicalese, R. Weatherly, J. Sherrill, R. Bolling, K. Forbes, R. Grabowski, K. Ring, and D. Seidel. *A Distributed Multi-Language Architecture for Large Unmanned Ground Vehicles.* Proceedings of the 2008 Annual ACM SIGAda International Conference on Ada. October 2008.

[21] Tokeneer. Retrieved from http://www.adacore.com/home/products/sparkpro/tokeneer/

Author Index

Bail, William 1

Black, Paul E. 31

Bradley, Peter J. 37

Bu, Lei 53

Cheng, Albert M. K. 13

Cicalese, Cindy 9

de la Puente, Juan A. 37

Fong, Elizabeth 31

Garfinkel, Simson 31

Jemli, Mamdouh 23

Lane, Chris 11

Leslie, Richard F. 31

Li, Xuandong 53

Li, You 53

McCormick, John W. 5

McGraw, Gary 31

Moore, Brad J. 41

Pettit IV, Robert G. 7

Ras, Jim 13

Rosen, Jean-Pierre 3, 23

Schmidt, Richard B. 33

Schonberg, Edmond 63

Sherill, Joel 9

Sward, Ricky E. 9, 71

Wagoner, Larry 31

Wang, Linzhang 53

Weatherly, Richard 9, 35

Williams, Jeff 31

Yang, Lu 53

Zamorano, Juan 37

Zhao, Jianhua 53

ACM's Annual International Conference On Ada and Related Technologies: Engineering Safe, Secure, and Reliable Software

Fairfax, Virginia, USA
(Suburb of Washington DC, USA)
October 24-28, 2010
Sponsored by ACM SIGAda

Exhibitors Guide

Industrial Support by:

Founded in 1994, AdaCore is the leading provider of commercial software solutions for Ada, the state-of-the-art programming language designed for large, long-lived applications where safety, security, and reliability are critical. AdaCore's flagship product is the GNAT Pro development environment, which comes with expert on-line support and is available on more platforms than any other Ada technology. AdaCore has an extensive world-wide customer base; see www.adacore.com/home/company/customers/ for further information.

Ada and GNAT Pro see a growing usage in high-integrity and safety-certified applications, including commercial aircraft avionics, military systems, air traffic management/control, railway systems and medical devices, and in security-sensitive domains such as financial services.

AdaCore has North American headquarters in New York and European headquarters in Paris. www.adacore.com

North American Office

104 Fifth Avenue, 15th floor
New York, NY 10011
USA
Toll-free tel.
+1-877-SUP-GNAT (1-877-787-4628)
+1-866-SUP-4ADA (1-866-787-4232)
Tel. +1 212 620 7300
Fax +1 212 807 0162
Email: sales@adacore.com

European Office

46 rue d'Amsterdam
75009 Paris
FRANCE
Tel. +33 1 49 70 67 16
Fax +33 1 49 70 05 52
Email: sales@adacore.com

Ellidiss Software is a leading supplier of software tools to international organisations in aerospace, space, transport, defence and academia. Technologies supported by the tools include AADL, UML 2.0, HRT-HOOD, Requirements Analysis, and Software Method Prototyping. The company maintains its leading position through its involvement in standards committees and R & D projects, and by close cooperation with key organisations such as the European Space Agency, Ada Language organisations - SIGAda and Ada Europe, together with key Aerospace organisations worldwide.

UK Office

TNI Europe Ltd
Triad House
Mountbatten Court
Worrall Street
Congleton
Cheshire
UK
CW12 1DT
Tel:+44(0)1260 291449

European Office

TNI Europe Ltd
Ellidiss Technologies
24 quai de la douane
29200 Brest
France
Phone: +33 (0)298 451 870
Mobile: +33 (0)626 466 536
Email: pierre.dissaux@ellidiss.com

MathWorks is the leading developer of mathematical computing software. Engineers and scientists worldwide rely on its products to accelerate the pace of discovery, innovation, and development. Polyspace® code verifiers detect and prove the absence of overflow, divide-by-zero, out-of-bounds array access, and other run-time errors in source code. Polyspace uses static analysis that is formal methods based (with abstract interpretation) to verify C/C++ or Ada. You can use it to perform static code analysis and code verification of embedded software that is handwritten or generated. Polyspace can also be used to check compliance to coding standards and to measure software quality. For more information, please visit www.mathworks.com

MathWorks
3 Apple Hill Dr.
Natick, MA 01760
508-647-7000
www.mathworks.com

For more than thirty years, LDRA has developed and driven the market for software that automates code analysis and software testing for safety-, mission-, security- and business- critical markets. Working with clients to achieve early error identification and full compliance with industry standards, LDRA traces requirements through static and dynamic analysis to unit testing and verification for a wide variety of hardware and software platforms. Boasting a worldwide presence, LDRA is headquartered in the UK with subsidiaries in the United States and India and an extensive distributor network. For more information on the LDRA tool suite, please visit: www.ldra.com.

LDRA Technology, Inc
Lake Amir Office Park
1250 Bayhill Drive, Suite # 360
San Bruno, CA 94066
Tel: (650) 583 8880
Fax: (650) 583 8881
E-mail: info@ldra.com
Web: www.ldra.com